WHOLEHEARTED
Living the Life You Were Created to Live

Leslie Nease

WestBow
PRESS
A DIVISION OF THOMAS NELSON

WestBow Press books may be ordered through booksellers or by contacting:

WestBow Press
A Division of Thomas Nelson
1663 Liberty Drive
Bloomington, IN 47403
www.westbowpress.com
1-(866) 928-1240

Scripture quotations are taken from the Holy Bible, New Living Translation, copyright ©1996, 2004, 2007. Used by permission of Tyndale House Publishers, Inc., Carol Stream, Illinois 60188. All rights reserved.

Cover design by: Chris Comstock of C2Pictures.com
Photography by: Nathan Abplanalp Photography

ISBN: 978-1-4497-8515-4 (sc)
ISBN: 978-1-4497-8516-1 (hc)
ISBN: 978-1-4497-8514-7 (e)

Library of Congress Control Number: 2013902632

Printed in the United States of America

WestBow Press rev. date: 2/13/2013

Dedication

To my husband, Rod.
Thank you for believing in me when I did not.
Your love, devotion, faithfulness and strength have
been God's greatest blessing in my life. Your constant
and unconditional love has helped shape me, encourage
me and given me the ability to trust again.
Words cannot express how deep my love is for you.

Endorsements

Wholehearted is a joyful and inspirational read from start to finish! Leslie Nease combines heartwarming true life stories with sound doctrinal principles that reach both the heart and the mind. I was encouraged, convicted, challenged, and strengthened. I strongly recommend this book for everyone who wants a closer walk with God.

Dr. Tony Beam
Vice-President for Student Services and
Director of the Christian Worldview Center at North Greenville University
Radio Host of Christian Worldview Today on Christian Talk 660

In her powerful new book, Leslie Nease walks us through what to expect once God performs spiritual "heart surgery" on us. With humility, honesty and lifelong-friend-relatability, she weaves her own incredible story of God's tireless pursuit of her entire heart with Scriptural truth that will encourage and edify yours. No matter where you are in your journey of faith, you will find encouragement as Leslie reminds us who God is: the Healer of our hearts, the Sustainer of a life dedicated to Him, and our only hope for living a fully *wholehearted* life!

Lindsay McCaul
Christian Recording Artist
"Come Rest" - as heard on His Radio

Wholehearted is not just a book — it's a real, honest-to-goodness love journey that will move you deeply. Leslie Nease pours her life out on each page with tender courage to point you toward the peaceful and purposeful life that each of us long for.

Gwen Smith
Author, Speaker, Worship Leader & Songwriter
Co-founder of Girlfriends in God

Leslie has a way of walking you through the foundations of faith that make you feel like you've just been on a road trip with a girlfriend. Wholehearted serves as the road map to the abundant life that you've always wanted.

Carol Davis
Christian Radio Host and Program Director at WMIT
Speaker and Writer

In her new book, *Wholehearted,* Leslie Nease effortlessly relates in a way that captivates and encourages even the most skeptical and suspicious heart among us. I urge everyone to take this opportunity to heal your weary heart with such sweet words of wisdom, grace, and kindness.

Courtney Yates
Fellow Former Fei Long Tribe Member, *Survivor China*, 2007 (when the show first started, it was obvious Leslie and Courtney were put on the same tribe because of their differences. But after spending time together in the jungles of China, they have become very close friends)

Leslie has written an inspiring and encouraging book, drawing deeply from the trials, struggles and disappointments of her own journey, that clearly shows that life's ultimate victory is only found in Christ. If you, like many, are weighed down by the baggage from your "old" life that you allowed into your "new" life and simply cannot seem to get free from it...be encouraged. *Wholehearted* is the book for you!

Pastor Steve McCranie
The Church Without Walls
Gastonia, NC

Leslie gets right to the "heart of the matter" by sharing her heart in her new book, Wholehearted. The analogy she uses between a physical heart patient and a spiritual heart patient really brought this book alive for me! Even if you've been on a journey with Jesus for years or if you have never heard of Him, there is something in this book that will stir and challenge your heart. Thank you, Leslie, for being yourself and sharing your story!

Brian Sumner
Afternoon Host/Promotions Director
His Radio

Table of Contents

Forward

Everyone has at least one *Leslie* in his or her life. Of course not the same exact *Leslie* but one with the same kind of heart. He or she is in your workplace, your school, your church, your family, or maybe even closer than you originally thought. The person may even be the reflection in your mirror.

She is someone who is restless at heart and trying to do the right thing, but is frustrated deep down because she knows she is living in two different worlds. She wants to live like she has a peaceful and purposed life, but she knows that something is still missing deep within.

I met my *Leslie*, the one who wrote this book, in a Bible study in her living room many years ago. I have watched her grow from having a frustrated, restless heart to a joyful heart. Truth be told, when she asked me to be her mentor I rather reluctantly accepted the position. God prompted my heart to say, "yes," even while everything inside me was screaming, "But God, she is so different from me! How could this ever work?" Funny thing, though - it was one of the best decisions that I have ever made. God has brought Leslie from her living room to the position of sharing God's way of joy to an audience of millions.

At speaking events all over the country, we constantly hear, "I wish that others in my life had come to hear this message. I know it would encourage them as it has me. It is rare to hear that powerful combination of tender love and truth." That is the purpose of this book.

In the following pages, you will read how Leslie unpacks the meaning of Ezekiel 36:26-27: *"And I will give you a new heart, and I will put a new spirit in you. I will take out your stony, stubborn heart and give you a tender, responsive heart. And I will put my Spirit in you so that you will follow my decrees and be careful to obey my regulations."*

Are you ready for a fresh faith journey? One that will point you to the grace, peace, healing and purpose of God that is uniquely designed for you? Get comfortable and prepare to experience heart-rest and joy that is higher, deeper and wider than you've ever known. Prepare to live whole heartedly.

With Great Love for "My" Leslie and for Yours,
Linda Reppert
Mentor, Ministry Coordinator

Chapter One

Wholehearted

I will give them hearts that recognize me as the LORD.
They will be my people and I will be their God, for they
will return to me wholeheartedly. —Jeremiah 24:7

I spent over twenty years of my life trying to be someone I was not. I sought the approval and love of others only to find out that their love was conditional, temporary and unsatisfying. I did not understand that my longing for significance went much deeper than I could imagine.

In 1986, during my senior year in high school, my heart was beating out of my chest the day they announced the Senior Superlatives over the loudspeaker. I so desperately wanted to be voted "Most Likely to..." or "Best..." and as they read the list of winners one by one over the loudspeakers, I could barely contain my excitement as they announced *"Leslie Shade: Friendliest!"* I had a spring in my step and held my head high the rest of the day. Oh, how desperate I was to be liked! And now I knew it for sure: they liked me. They *really* liked me!

A few weeks later, I was at a party and there were a bunch of popular guys there who were standing around talking. I walked up to say hello and they all greeted me, "Leslie! Congratulations on winning friendliest!" I smiled big and pretended like I was humble about it, but inside I was beaming with pride. My joy was cut short in an instant though when one of the wrestlers yelled out, "Well, we all know how *friendly* you are, Leslie – it's no surprise you won!" They elbowed one another in the ribs and laughed in unison.

I knew what they meant. I was friendly, alright, but not the kind of friendly that one would be proud of being. I had made some pretty horrific choices in high school and some of those guys were among those with whom I made those very choices. My heart sank and I walked away in tears, ashamed of who I was and embarrassed that my choices had led me to this dark place of embarassment and humiliation.

Ouch. It hurt to be confronted with the reality of my behavior. It hurt even more because someone else pointed it out. This was the first time I felt like someone saw through my charade… and it was incredibly painful. Unfortunately, it would not be the last time my shame would be exposed.

When I first met my husband, Rod, in the summer of 1988, he was coming to town to visit his best friend, whom I was dating at the time. We were in college in West Virginia. Rod and his friends had arrived early in the morning and I was fast asleep in my boyfriend's apartment after a very sordid night of partying. I heard that the guys all came in and snickered and looked at me as I laid there on the couch, fast asleep. I knew that it was the first time Rod had ever seen me, but it wasn't until last year (twenty-four years later) that I asked him what he did when he saw me on the couch that morning. Somehow, I knew he was not the kind of guy who would have snickered and stared like the others did.

I was not prepared for what he told me. Rod said he walked over, took the covers and covered me up. Tears stung as they fell down my face after he told me this. I realized that God has given me an amazing man to walk beside me in this life. A man who, from the very beginning, covered my shame and loved me for who I was, not for what I could give him. He saw potential in me and believed in me.

I am not proud at all of who I was in my past, and honestly if I were to attend a class reunion, the people from high school would never believe I am the same person! I look the same on the outside (well, besides a few pounds), but I am not the same person at all on the inside. I can tell these incredibly painful stories to you now because I know that I am a new person – completely changed and living a wholehearted life from the inside out! But it was not always that way.

Having someone believe in me had a life-changing effect on me – and I am so thankful that not only did my Rod believe in me, but God did, too. All my life I thought God was angry with me. It changed my life when I realized that He loved me just the way I was but He loved me so much that He would not allow me to stay that way. He had more for my life and He knew that my heart would eventually change and my life would never be the same. Are you someone who needs to hear this, too? *God is not mad at you.* He loves you and He has plans for your life that go far beyond anything you could ever imagine! He believes in you.

King David believed in his son, Solomon, like that. He had some hopeful and powerful advice for him when he was advising Solomon on how to lead Israel, as he was next in line for the throne. Here's what King David told his son:

"So now, with God as our witness, and in the sight of all Israel—the LORD's assembly—I give you this charge. Be careful to obey all the commands of the LORD your God, so that you may continue to possess this good land and leave it to your children as a permanent inheritance. And Solomon, my son, learn to know the God of your ancestors intimately. Worship and serve Him with your whole heart and a willing mind. For the LORD sees every heart and knows every plan and thought. If you seek Him, you will find him. But if you forsake Him, he will reject you forever. So take this seriously. The LORD has chosen you to build a Temple as his sanctuary. Be strong, and do the work." (1 Chronicles 28:8-10)

Solomon must have taken much of what his father said to him to heart because he ended up being a very wise and powerful King. It's some of the greatest advice I've had the pleasure of reading in the Bible. David knew that the most important thing in his son's life would be that he would obey God, know God, worship God and seek God – **wholeheartedly**. These are excellent words for all of us.

You might know the joy of redemption like I do… or you could possibly be worn out from half-hearted attempts to live a joy-filled life on your own. Perhaps you are in a good place with God… or maybe you have been trying and failing repeatedly to be the person you desperately want to be, but you feel like you are living a lie. Oh, my friend, you have picked up the right book! I can totally to relate to the struggles we all face and I pray God will give you answers and encouragement as we spend time together seeking Him wholeheartedly. He does want you to live the life you were created to live – and you can live it – with His help.

In the pages you are about to read, you will find the answers to many of the questions you may be asking yourself:

- Is there more to this life? Is this all there is?
- My heart doesn't always want to obey God. Is it even possible?
- Why can't I seem to find peace in my life?
- I said a prayer to ask Jesus in my heart, so why don't I feel "saved"?
- I go to church, I volunteer and I wear myself out trying to impress God – do you think He notices?
- I have sinned so much. Is God ever going to be able to forgive me?

These are all questions I had prior to my life changing "spiritual heart transplant." The unfulfilment in my life was a symptom of undiagnosed heart disease, but not a physical disease; more of a spiritual one. Until I stopped *trying* so hard to be good and began to realize I was *dying*, I was stuck in a rut of misery within an empty existence while I always felt like a fraud and a failure. My "outside" life looked just fine, but inside I knew something was missing. And I just couldn't put my finger on it. Maybe you know exactly what I'm talking about.

Seeking God wholeheartedly can be a difficult thing to do

with all of the distractions and deceptions in the world today, though. It can be challenging but it is the most rewarding thing in the world! But before you can begin your search, it is a good idea to understand that your search for Him can lead you to try to fill that void in your life with things that are not ever going to fill you up – like I had done, instead those things will leave you feeling empty and disappointed.

I don't know where this finds you or what you've tried to fill your empty heart up with. Maybe it is an addiction, a relationship, a position at work, popularity, a reputation or something else that is the temporary object of your misled attempts to be fulfilled – but if God is not the object of your affection, we will find something (or someone) else to try to fill our emptiness. Only God can complete us and empower us to live the life we were created to live. Being conscious of this can be life changing. How do I know? I've experienced it. I'm living it. Living with purpose and peace. Beyond what I ever imagined. You can too.

As we begin this journey together, let me introduce you to my new friend, Jeannie. Jeannie is a beautiful woman I met while doing research for this book. I know God intentionally crossed our paths for a very specific reason, and one of those reasons is you. Yes, you. I believe that her story will both inspire and challenge you...

Chapter Two

Heart Failure

This sickness will not end in death. No, it is for God's glory, so that the Son of God may receive glory through it. — John 11:4

Jeannie Fuller awoke in the wee hours of the morning on March 3, 2007 and slowly lifted herself from the comfort of her fluffy pillows and her familiar, warm bed. As she sat on the edge of her mattress, she glanced over and saw her husband, Chip, sleeping peacefully. It was good to see him resting. He had not done much of that in the past couple of years as he stood by her, praying for her and rarely leaving her side as she fought for her life.

Jeannie knew she loved Chip when she married him over sixteen years ago, but after seeing his deep and abiding love for her during this incredible trial, she knew she would never question his love or devotion for her again. Tears fell down her face as she gazed out the window and witnessed the most astonishing and breathtaking sunrise she had ever seen. She was alive and everything was beautiful – more beautiful than ever. It was an overwhelming moment that, even today, she recalls with tears in her eyes.

Her journey began over two and a half years prior, in September of 2004. She was a happy, busy mother of three. Chip was the associate pastor at a local church. She had spent the day driving her kids to their practices, cleaning, and grocery shopping. It was her day off from work and she had a lot to do, as is typical in the life of a busy mom. Everything seemed normal except that she had been feeling a burning sensation in her chest. Dizziness was also creeping in and as the day progressed, so did her anxiety.

She mentioned the burning sensation in her chest to Chip and he dismissed it by saying, "Oh, that must be the meatball sub you ate for lunch." She agreed and took an antacid. After about twenty minutes, she realized something was terribly wrong. The burning was worsening and her dizziness was almost unbearable. She told Chip it was time to take her to the emergency room and immediately went to sit in the car and wait for him. Although Chip had not thought much of her symptoms up to this point, he quickly realized something serious was going on when his wife acted like this. Numbing fear raced through him like a wave of hot, paralyzing wind.

The nurses at the hospital had an extremely difficult time getting an accurate blood pressure on Jeannie. Her pulse was racing at 250 beats per minute. A nurse by profession, Jeannie knew this meant trouble. After running some tests, the doctors delivered the news the Fullers were not expecting. Her heart was failing. Jeannie had a heart condition that was presumably caused by a virus or an autoimmune disorder. The doctors determined she was in complete heart block and her heart would go into frequent and dangerous, life-threatening arrhythmias if they did not do something immediately. She would require a diffibulator/pacemaker. The doctors performed the procedure and within days Jeannie was released from the hospital. Jeannie knew that everything would be fine now and believed that she would heal completely and return to her normal life. She did not have time for this! So she kept herself busy and continued to do the things that busy moms do.

That is exactly what she did for about fourteen months. But Chip noticed her energy levels were not where they used to be and she was spending a lot more time in bed. The doctors changed her medications several times, but nothing seemed to be working. By January of 2006, the doctor told Jeannie that her heart was not getting better, but instead was getting much worse. He told her that she was going to be referred to a specialist to be evaluated for a heart transplant.

Shock and denial crept over her. Even though the doctor was serious, Jeannie believed the heart she was born with would heal and she would be fine. She took the news in stride. Chip felt like *he* needed a heart transplant at that moment. He was heartbroken at this news, but they believed in the depths of their souls that God was going to heal her. They would not even say the word "transplant" and instead, called it the "T" word after this conversation. Their faith was unshakeable.

Jeannie did not get better, though. For two years, she kept hoping for a miracle cure and though her energy was lessening by the day, she continued to believe her healing would come. She was living in denial, but her denial was not that she did not believe her condition was dire, because there was no denying how she was feeling. She just did not want to believe that she would need a transplant. I have actually talked with several heart transplant recipients and apparently, this is a very common reaction. It is a difficult reality to face. Much to her dismay, she wound up on the transplant list by September of 2006 and was admitted into the hospital where she needed continuous IV drip to sustain her heart function. She was moved to the ICU, placed on the highest status and was a priority for any matching donor hearts. Her miraculous healing was indeed on its way, but it would look nothing like what she hoped for so long.

Jeannie was able to spend Christmas with her family, but after the holidays she was taken back to the hospital and admitted indefinitely. The doctors considered implanting a ventricular assist device (VAD) to take over the work of her heart, but she had a fever and it prevented the surgery. She thanks God for this because she knows that if the device had been put in, she would have been taken off the transplant list for months until she recuperated from the open-heart procedure and she would have missed out on receiving her perfect, new heart.

On January 26, things got very grim for Jeannie. She prayed silently to the Lord, "I do not want to leave my family, but I surrender to You tonight. If that is Your will, so be it." She was too weak to fight and depended on God for her strength every single moment. Her church and her family were praying that God would sustain her and bring a new heart. On February 2, the cherished news came: they had found a heart for Jeannie. They began testing to determine if it was the right heart and found that indeed, it was. On February 3, 2007, Jeannie Fuller had the seven-hour surgery and received her new heart.

The extensive process of recovery began. Almost immediately after waking from her surgery, Jeannie's thoughts began to drift to the donor's family. In a recent conversation, she said, "I remember feeling overwhelmed that someone would give me their heart. It's so hard to describe the feelings I have toward the donor. I was and still am so humbled that someone would give me the gift of life."

Now, here she was, four weeks later, and she was waking up in her familiar bed with the sounds and smells of home for the first time with her new heart. Oh, how she had missed her home. The sounds of her children playing, the hustle and bustle of everyday life, the familiar smell of clean laundry and her favorite potpourri she liked to have sitting out in the living room. The sterile hospital smells were nauseating to her and the sound of her heart monitor was enough to drive anyone out of their mind! She even threw away everything that reminded her of those tough days – shampoos, lotions and even the sweatshirt Chip wore frequently while they were in the hospital. It was all behind her now. She took in a deep breath and closed her eyes to thank God for this gift that was steadily beating in her chest. The scar would be a painful, yet beautiful remembrance of the surgery that saved her life. She was now waking up to her new life and it was so very sweet.

The tough road ahead would require perseverance and determination, but Jeannie was up for the challenge. Her complete trust in her Heavenly Father had intensified over the past couple of years. She felt closer to Him than ever. She had heard stories of people who had been through difficult times and had grown in their faith through the trial, and now she was counted as one of them. Jeannie believed the breathtaking sunrise that morning was a gift from her Father in Heaven; a sweet reminder that He was with her, guiding her and sustaining her.

Jeannie raised herself up off the bed and began to make her way, slowly, to her children's rooms. She could hardly wait to see their sweet faces! She and Chip had returned home from the hospital the night before around midnight and it was all they could do to keep from waking up the children in the middle of the night. It had been so long since they had felt like a "normal" family. Chip heard her shuffling cautiously across the bedroom and came running to her side.

Together, they entered the first bedroom. Jeannie was overwhelmed and as tears stung her cheeks, she gazed at her angelic little girl. She could hardly wait until she woke up so she could braid her hair and snuggle with her like they used to do all the time. Down the hall, they slowly peered into the bedroom of their son. How they he had grown in the past two months! She could hardly wait to feel his sweet arms around her neck. She and Chip walked quietly to her eldest daughter's room and was overjoyed to see her resting peacefully in her bed. She wondered if she was resting easier now that her mother was home. Sometimes the eldest instinctively takes on more responsibility when the mother is away. She looked more grown up than ever.

Jeannie looked around the house and saw that everything was so clean and orderly. Her heart was full of gratitude as the faces and names of people who had come alongside of her family through this long and difficult trial came to mind. They had made sure her family was cared for and that her precious children had clean clothes, an orderly home, hot meals and warm hugs. Such selflessness! How could she ever thank them?

Over the next few weeks, her physical healing was demanding to say the least. She recalls even going up the stairs at home was a difficult task. Jeannie recalls, "We started with one stair and worked our way up. I remember getting to eight and raising my hands in victory! I felt like *Rocky*. This was truly a victory moment for us. It took me about twelve weeks before I could walk up the stairs!" I can almost hear the *Rocky* theme song, can't you?

Within a year, Jeannie was physically about 75% overall. She was probably at about 98% by the end of two years. In order to keep her body from rejecting her new heart, she must take several pills twice per day. She also must get a heart biopsy on a staggered interval schedule for the rest of her life. During this biopsy they insert a catheter into her jugular vein and go down into her heart and snip a little piece to send to pathology to see if she is rejecting the heart. All of this is what she calls "post heart transplant life." And it is worth it.

I had the pleasure of meeting Jeannie when I began research for this book. About a year before, I had been approached by a group of women in Washington state to speak at their annual women's conference. They asked me to share four messages based on the scriptures from Ezekiel 36:26-27. As I meditated on these vereses, *"And I will give you a new heart, and I will put a new spirit in you. I will take out your stony, stubborn heart and give you a tender, responsive heart. And I will put my Spirit in you so that you will follow my decrees and be careful to obey my regulations,"* I realized that when we put our faith and trust in Jesus Christ, He doesn't just come into our heart, He actually gives us a new one!

I started interviewing people who had a physical heart transplant to share their stories with me and began to see some incredible parallels. Jeannie and I connected instantly and I was in awe of her faith and positive outlook after having been through so much. I knew right away that I wanted to know more about her and that her story would be the one I would share. Her faith, combined with her incredible love for Jesus and her determination to fight have really inspired me.

I had a dear friend who has since passed away tell me there is no such thing as coincidences. He called them "God-cidences". I believe it is a *God-cidence* that the parallels between the spiritual and physical heart transplant are so striking. I prepared four sessions for the women's conference based on Ezekiel 36:26–27 and the response was overwhelming. Women's lives were changed for eternity. That was when I knew I had to write this down and share with as many people as I could all that God taught me through this process.

There are so many people who are living the Christian life from the outside in – trying to change their behavior instead of allowing God to change their heart. I was counted among those people for over twenty years; attending church, professing faith in Christ, but completely miserable down deep. I knew something was missing, but I did not know what it was. I thought Christianity was a game and I was pretty good at it, honestly. But God finally revealed to me my true condition, and like Jeannie, I could not deny it anymore.

Chapter Three
Spiritual Heart Transplant

"And I will give you a new heart, and I will put a new spirit in you. I will take out your stony, stubborn heart and give you a tender, responsive heart." -Ezekiel 36:26

When I first talked to Jeannie on the phone, I knew I had made a friend for life. She loved Jesus and her sweet spirit and willingness to allow me to share her story with you made me realize that God was the One knitting us together. Her heart transplant story inspired me and made me realize how precious life is. Her willingness to be vulnerable and her openness to share her struggles, victories, and hurdles with me made me want to be more vulnerable. That is how God works. He uses each of us to inspire one another. Her story reminded me of my own heart transplant. But it is not the kind you might be thinking of. It was more of a spiritual one.

Let me pause here and take a moment to clarify that when I speak about our spiritual heart, I am not speaking of the one in the center of your chest that beats and pushes blood through your body. Here's a good explanation from *Easton's Bible Dictionary*:

> "According to the Bible, the heart is the center not only of spiritual activity, but also of all the operations of human life. The heart is also the seat of the conscience (Romans 2:15). It is naturally wicked (Genesis 8:21), and hence it contaminates the whole life and character (Matthew 12:34; 15:18, Ecclesiastes 8:11 and Psalm 73:7) Hence the heart must be changed, regenerated (Ezekiel 36:26, Ezekiel 11:19, Psalm 51:10) before a man can *willingly* obey God."

Jeannie's problem was that she had a diseased physical heart. She was in denial for over two years and while she denied, she almost died. Her heart was failing and her family would have lost her without a heart transplant. I cannot help but recognize that we are in the exact same place, spiritually speaking. When we first hear that our spiritual heart is diseased, our initial reaction is just like Jeannie's – we usually go into denial. "I'm fine. I don't need help. I am a good person. The way I live my life is proof you don't need God to be good." But is that really the truth? Our hearts are born sin-filled – a disease that, according to Romans 6:23 leaves a death sentence if left untreated. The verse says, *"For the wages of sin is death, but the free gift of God is eternal life through Christ Jesus our Lord."* Therein lies the Good News! We have a chance at life – through Christ Jesus, our Lord.

This leads me to my next parallel. Jeannie's heart required a donor. She struggled desperately – especially in the beginning

– with the realization that someone had to die in order for her to live. In her words, "I felt so unworthy to receive someone's heart because I was reminded that someone had to die in order for me to have life. But then I remember that someone had already done that. Jesus, 2000 years ago, died so that I could live eternally." Jeannie's donor did not die specifically for her to have a new heart and probably would have prefered to stay alive, but Jesus willingly and lovingly allowed His life to be taken so yours and my spiritual heart could be made right with God. He died willingly, knowing that it was the only way. In order for us to live, He had to die. The wages of sin is death – and He took our death-punishment on Himself.

I am not sure about you, but that makes me feel the exact same way that Jeannie felt about her donor. I feel unworthy. I feel overwhelmed. But I am so thankful, and I do not want to waste a single moment. I will explain more about why Jesus died and why that matters to you in greater detail in the next two chapters, so stay with me!

Jeannie said, "As a Christian, I always wanted to be obedient to my Savior but after the transplant, I have a passion and more of a sense of urgency to be about my Savior's business. I know the reality of life. It is short. We are not promised tomorrow. " I sense that Jeannie is living her life with a new determination. She has tremendous gratitude for her donor's sacrifice and does not want to waste a single moment. When you realize someone died in your place so you could live, you instinctively live more determined, with more passion and with more purpose than ever. Oh, how I can relate to this! I heard a quote the other day, "When your life has no central purpose, you are more vulnerable to fall prey to petty fears, worries and depressive thoughts." That was me, B.C. (Before Christ). Now that I know Christ, my life is filled with purpose and passion. It is truly amazing how He has transformed me. I was a mess. But my "mess" has now been changed into God's "message."

The "life after transplant" that Jeannie is now accustomed to has a few comparisons to our "life after transplant," too. She must take several medications twice per day in order to keep her body from rejecting her heart. I can tell you with complete certainty that I do the same thing, but it looks much different. Instead of ingesting medicine, I ingest the Word of God and spend time in prayer with my Father in Heaven. I do this because my flesh (the old me – my natural, sinful nature) wants to reject this new heart desperately. Paul describes this battle perfectly in Romans 7:18-25a:

> "And I know that nothing good lives in me, that is, in my sinful nature. I want to do what is right, but I can't. I want to do what is good, but I don't. I don't want to do what is wrong, but I do it anyway. But if I do what I don't want to do, I am not really the one doing wrong; it is sin living in me that does it. I have discovered this principle of life—that when I want to do what is right, I inevitably do what is wrong. I love God's law with all my heart. But there is another power within me that is at war with my mind. This power makes me a slave to the sin that is still within me. Oh, what a miserable person I am! Who will free me from this life that is dominated by sin and death? Thank God! The answer is in Jesus Christ our Lord."

Can you relate to Paul's struggle? It is one we all have as believers in Jesus Christ. It can be overwhelming at times. Those are usually the times when we are not "taking our spiritual medicine – God's Word and fellowship with Him – on time." In all seriousness, our spiritual health depends on us spending time with God daily. Notice the last sentence in that scripture – *the answer is in Jesus Christ our Lord*. If we are not spending time with Him daily, learning to trust Him, we will begin to notice symptoms of heart failure. These symptoms include worry, fears, doubt and discouragement. When I begin to have a lot of these symptoms, I know what I need to do. And I can usually trace it back to me being negligent of my time with God. We feed our bodies when they are hungry, right? Well, our spirit gets hungry, too, and we feed it by spending time with our Lord.

Jeannie's heart biopsy at staggered intervals is also something she must endure for her "post transplant life." The doctors are checking for signs of rejection. This is a painful but necessary process she knows she must undergo. I look at this as time we spend being real, open, and honest with someone godly, like a spiritual mentor or friend. These are people whom God places in our lives for accountability. They are more mature in their faith and they have a gift of teaching and discipleship. They ask us the tough questions. It can be painful at times. It is a real struggle to go through the kind of "heart biopsy" that a mentor can offer, but it can be life saving. Our mentors are sent by God to check for signs of rejection. Is our flesh winning out? Or is our heart healthy and strong? Oh, I could go on and on about the benefits of a mentor in your life, but I will wait until chapter eight, when I will give you practical steps and biblical guidance on how to form mentoring relationships in your life. For now, I just wanted you to see the incredible comparison!

Notice, as well, that Jeannie had a long period of time before she was working at full capacity with her new heart. Her first year was a very slow recovery process. Remember her "victory" on the stairs? She was thankful she had made it to eight steps and held her hands up in celebration! As a new believer with a new heart, we must realize we are not going to have all the answers to all the tough theological questions that people may ask. We do not make the right decision every time we are faced with a tough choice. We may not know how to pray yet. We may have a hard time initially with reaching out to other believers for accountability. It takes time to acclimate to our new heart. It takes time, intention and determination – much like the time, intention and determination Jeannie showed in her recovery process. We should not put unrealistic expectations on ourselves. Every step in the right direction is a small victory and we should not be afraid to celebrate! Eventually, we will grow in our faith more and more. Our new heart will become such a part of us that we will know exactly what Paul meant when he declared in 2 Corinthians 5:17, *"Anyone who belongs to Christ has become a new person. The old life is gone; a new life has begun!"*

I'm so thrilled to have you on this journey with me. I cannot begin to tell you how much God has blessed me as I have been studying God's Word in relation to this book and how blessed I feel as I've realized how important it is that we recognize that God is the one who changes us. It is not up to us! The heart of the matter is that we all need a new heart. We cannot live the

Christian life victoriously unless our heart has been changed completely by Jesus Christ.

In the next couple of chapters, I will share my personal journey with you about my "spiritual heart transplant" and what led up to this life-changing moment. But I wanted to introduce you to my new friend, Jeannie, first because her story inspired me and gave me such a beautiful picture of how much God loves us and cares for us.

I do not know where you stand spiritually, but I know beyond a shadow of a doubt that you are reading this book for a very important purpose. Remember, there are no coincidences. If you are already a spiritual heart transplant recipient, I pray this book will be an encouragement to you and will help clarify any questions or thoughts you might have, or perhaps it will help equip you to share your story with others. If you are someone who may have just realized your diagnosis of spiritual heart disease, I pray you will not give denial access into your mind, as Jeannie did and as I did for so many years. Read the pages of this book with an open heart and allow God's truth and His Word complete access. Consider it a biopsy of sorts. My prayer is that by the time you put this book down, you will be a new creation – someone transformed from the inside out and a proud owner of a new heart, compliments of Jesus.

Chapter Four

My Heart Condition

*"People may be right in their own eyes, but
the Lord examines their heart."*
Proverbs 21:2

The first time I heard about Jesus was at a revival at a huge
church in Martinsburg, West Virginia with my sister and
my mother when I was about ten years old. The lively evangelist
was shouting at the top of his lungs while sweat beads fell off his
brow. He was very passionate about what he was preaching and
he seemed urgent in his pleas as he zealously shared about Jesus.
Up to that point, the only time I'd ever heard about Jesus was
in the song from Kris Kristopherson, *"Why Me, Lord?"* where
he sings, *"Lord, help me Jesus!"* I had always wondered who this
"Jesus" guy was and why he was the only one who could help
Mr. Kristopherson. But on this night, I was being taught a very
powerful lesson about Jesus and frankly, I was scared stiff.

It was also the first night I ever heard about heaven and hell. My mind was whirling and my heart was racing. I was terrified as the evangelist told ghastly details of the suffering, flames, and horror of hell. It was a place I never wanted to go. When he said all I had to do was ask Jesus into my heart at the end of the service, I went running up to the front to say whatever I needed to say to avoid going there. My mother and sister both went forward that night in the church to say a prayer so they wouldn't go to hell, either.

I was very relieved when the older woman who prayed with me told me that since I prayed the prayer I was no longer going to go to hell. I did not really understand who Jesus was or why I had to ask him into my heart. I didn't know much about God, didn't even know what sin was except I knew it was not good. I knew that I had done a lot of really bad things and I wondered if the things I had done would ever really be forgiven just like that loud preacher had said.

As I tossed and turned that night in my bed, I was still trembling. One thing bothered me about God. The evangelist at church told us that He was our "Heavenly Father." I had two fathers leave me in the past, and the thought of another leaving was more than I could bear. Would this Heavenly Father leave me, too? I had always wondered if I had done something wrong to make my daddies leave. My biological father and my mother divorced when I was just a baby, but I saw him occasionally when he would come and visit us. I really loved him but did not see him very often. My mother married my stepfather who was like a father to me when I was very young, but they divorced when I was in the second grade. I was devastated. The thought of having yet another father was scary to me. *What if he left, too?*

Although it was the night the name of Jesus first became familiar to me, it would take years before I truly knew Him and had a real relationship with Him. I suppose you could say that was the moment my "God radar" began to go off in my life. Before this happened, I was not aware of who He was or that He even existed. It was the beginning of a long journey to a new heart and a new life that God would eventually lavish on me.

Several months after that revival, my mother re-married our stepfather. He struggled with alcohol in the past, which was one of the reasons they divorced in the first place, but my mom told him about Jesus and he ended up saying that same prayer to receive Him into his heart, too. I remember being so glad because I really loved him. I always called him "Daddy," even after they were divorced. He was the only father I ever really knew and having him back in my life felt pretty amazing. He was no longer drinking and they seemed to be back on track again.

My stepfather was in the military and right after they remarried, we were stationed to a desert area in the southern part of California. We joined a church and my parents began serving in the bus ministry. Every Saturday we would venture out and go door to door, asking people to come to church, giving the kids candy and telling them we'd pick them up on Sunday morning, so if their parents did not want to come they would still have a ride. We did this for years and I enjoyed doing it because it made me feel important.

What we did not realize was that the church we were attending was very legalistic. What that means is that they were very focused on "behavior modification" but they did not teach much about God's love, grace and forgiveness. Since we were all so new to this church thing, we were willing to do whatever we were told and we did not realize that there were churches that were not teaching the Bible correctly. As far as we knew, a church was a church and if they taught from the Bible, we were good to go.

The church leadership told us that it was a sin against God for women to wear pants so we began wearing culottes and skirts all the time. We even wore culottes when we played games on the softball team. I have a distinct memory of getting put on restriction for a couple of weeks when I snuck some *Levi's* jeans out in my purse to the roller rink and changed when I got there. My parents figured out what I had done and were furious with me. *What if someone from church had seen me?*

We burned our secular music records in a bon-fire they hosted at the church where they told us of the sinfulness of all "devil music" on the radio. I remember watching my mom's eyes swell with tears as she threw her beloved *Elvis Presley* albums into the roaring fire. Then, we pitched out our television because we were told it was a tool of Satan and was to be avoided at all costs. We lived in constant fear of failing not only God, but also our church family.

My sister and I attended the Christian School at the church and our mother was a teacher there, as well. We would rarely escape the church or school campus. The temptations to sin seemed more pronounced when we ventured out into "the world." The members of this church were very controlling and the moment we would mess up in any way, I think they knew about it before we did. There was not much love going around, just rules on top of rules. I did not learn about how to have a relationship with Christ and my new Heavenly Father, only about the expectations of how I should behave and the resulting discipline when I did not live up to their demanding expectations.

When our eyes were finally opened and we left the church, we received anonymous hate mail from members for months. It was horrible! We were stalked and if we were ever seen out in public wearing pants, we were confronted with anonymous letters and phone calls. Once we were scorned for wearing bathing suits in our own backyard.

This became one of the most difficult and confusing experiences of my life. They called us sinners and heathens. Our best friends from the church came to our home with their Bibles in hand and told us that the pastor told them they were not allowed to be "unequally yoked" with unbelievers, so they could not be our friends anymore. We were rejected, humiliated, and ridiculed – mostly anonymously, but always from someone at that church. My idea of what church was all about was tainted, bitter, and not at all a picture of the true church that we read about in the New Testament. My heart was beginning to turn further and further away from God.

We moved to Okinawa, Japan in 1982 when I was just about to start high school. Somehow, my parents were still okay with the idea of going to church, but we did change denominations. I could not shake it though. I did not want to go. *All the hate. All the judgment. All the condemnation.* It was just more than I could handle. My heart was not into going to church or hearing about an angry, cranky God. I did not want this God for my

Heavenly Father. I always felt like a disappointment to Him anyways and it was wearing on me.

I figured out that I could just play the church game – like a charade. The dictionary defines a charade as, "a blatant pretense or deception, especially something so full of pretense as to be a travesty". Yes, that sounds about right. I would memorize Scriptures so my parents would be proud and think I was a good girl, but honestly, the Bible made no sense to me and reading it was pure torture. My heart was hard and unresponsive to the Bible. I showed up for youth group, went to church every time the doors opened. I pretended and counted the days until I was on my own and I would not have to pretend anymore. The people outside of the church were a lot easier for me to be around because I could just be myself. At church, I felt like a fraud, but by then I honestly thought everyone was playing the charade and that nobody really wanted to be there. We were just trying to stay out of hell by going through the motions, right? Wasn't everyone just wearing a mask?

I lived two lives at this point, and my heart was divided. I was the daughter of a church deacon, I was active in the youth group (though I was often making more trouble for the youth pastor than I was actually doing him any good), and I was always there when they needed help in the nursery. On the other hand, I was partying and drinking, smoking, and rebelling with boys. I made horrific choices for myself and I was absolutely miserable in the depths of my heart.

There was a girl who attended high school with me named Katrina who actually lived out her faith in a real way – it did not seem like a game to her. I would watch her sometimes. People were drawn to her sweet spirit and her genuine personality. She had a "special something" that everyone loved and respected. Later in my life I would realize that "special something" was the Holy Spirit, the Spirit of God in her, but at this point in my life I struggled because I knew I could not be like that. She was so well behaved and sweet. She actually seemed to enjoy reading her Bible and she had a smile that would light up the room. She wasn't a phony at all and she wasn't playing a game. Where was her mask? There was no judgment in the way she treated me. Katrina was the first person I can recall who actually showed me that Christianity is not living a life of duality. Being around her was very refreshing yet incredibly convicting for me.

My sinful behavior continued and even amplified when I went away to college. I swore I would never go to church again. No sense in feeling guilty anymore – I would have my own life! I did not want to answer to anyone and I was tired of pretending I was good when I knew I wasn't. Why try to please a Heavenly Father who was impossible to please? I was finally free!

Or so I thought.

My misery intensified as I began to drink more and more to numb the pain and embarrassment of the horrible decisions I was making in each and every college semester. I hated who I was, but I did not know how to be anyone else. I recall many of the wee hours in the morning where I would take "the walk of shame" across campus to return to my dorm after a night of partying and wrong choices with men. I had no respect for myself, and honestly, nobody else respected me either. I was getting quite a reputation on campus.

Then in the summer of 1988 I received news that was a complete shock and sent me into a tailspin. My roommate Patty had been killed in an automobile accident. I remember running up to her room and sobbing as I held her towel in my arms that she had just used after her shower that morning – it was still wet. This was surreal. It was so painful; I couldn't even get the sobs out. How could this happen? Was God mad at me? Was this punishment for everything I had done wrong? It was the first time I had even thought about God in a long time. Was she in heaven or hell? Why hadn't I asked her? Oh, my heart was breaking.

I met my husband in that very same summer. His father had been killed in an automobile accident a few years before so he was someone I could really talk to who understood my grief after losing Patty. I connected with him and felt safe with him, and I knew I was in love with him almost immediately.

Rod and I were married a year later and I was already four months pregnant. He initially thought we should get an abortion since we were so young, but I was not going to do that. I felt it was a miracle that I was even pregnant since a doctor had told me a year before that I would never have children because of an infection I came down with in my reproductive organs as a result of poor choices I had made earlier in my life. I also knew abortion was wrong and had witnessed a friend go through one earlier in life and I did not want to feel that kind of remorse and pain. My husband did not like abortion, but he was scared and he was not aware of the importance of the sanctity of life at this point in his life. He was trying to make a good decision, but I knew in my heart it was not the right decision for us to make.

I am so thankful that I didn't go along with what he initially thought we should do. He's thankful too now, by the way. At the time, we never could have known how God would use this precious little girl, our miracle, to change our lives.

During my pregnancy I told Rod that if he thought it was best we could give the baby up for adoption. Down deep I hoped he wouldn't actually want to, but I knew this would be the only way I could make certain she would be given a chance to live. As my due date loomed nearer, so did my love for my baby. I noticed Rod would put his hand on my belly and he would talk to the baby as my belly grew. I knew he was beginning to fall for our little one. When Stephanie was born in November of 1989, the doctor handed her to Rod and as he held our sweet little daughter, he wept. I knew he was in love and I knew he would not want to give her away. Our little family began that autumn night as the three of us snuggled together in the hospital bed.

A couple of years after Stephanie was born, we were blessed with another miracle and we named him Thomas (we call him Tommy). Again, we fell madly in love! Our children were so special to us. We loved them and began to think that maybe we should get them to church, a value our parents had always instilled in both of us. We did not have much desire for church ourselves, but we knew God was important and we knew our children should be raised in church. We would go sporadically but never consistently. It was just too much work and honestly it brought back some pretty bad memories for me. I figured that if we could just tell our kids if they believed in Jesus they wouldn't go to hell, we'd be fine. Who needs church anyway? All you have to do is say a prayer and you'll get out of hell, right?

I was so messed up.

Chapter Five

A Desperate Heart

And she made this vow: "O LORD of Heaven's Armies,
if you will look upon my sorrow and answer my prayer
and give me a son, then I will give him back to you. He
will be yours for his entire lifetime... -1 Samuel 1:11

In March of 1993 we were living in Newport News, Virginia. Stephanie, now four years old, came down with the chickenpox. At first, I didn't think much of it but after a day or so, I began to worry. Her temperature was 105 degrees. I took her to the emergency room where they told me it was "just the chickenpox." They sprayed disinfectant spray as we left and told us to stay home and give her ibuprofen for her fever. I was shocked at this, but then thought maybe I was over-reacting. The fever persisted in spite of ibuprofen. I took her back to the emergency room, but was sent home again and told not to make too much of it.

A couple of hours later, as I napped on my couch in the living room, Stephanie was resting in her bed down the hall and I had a dream. In my dream I was in her room, looking at her and she was sitting up in her bed with her arms reaching out to me, moaning and trying to cry but no sound was coming out. I woke up in a sweat and ran back only to find the exact scene from my dream being played out in real life. It was the most surreal thing I had ever been through and I was desperately trying to comfort her. She was in so much pain I couldn't even pick her up — she would scream when I touched her. She was burning hot and I was terrified.

I called the ambulance and they were there within minutes. They took her to the hospital and checked her in immediately. Her fever was up to 106 degrees. I was a complete wreck. What was going on? I was told that it was "just the chickenpox," but this seemed much more serious than they were letting on. She was swelling up and there was a huge bruise protruding from her right side. They had to cut her hospital identification wristband off twice and replace it because she was swelling up so much.

I knew the news was not good when five very serious looking doctors filled her room. They were somber as they gave me the news: "Stephanie is a very sick little girl. She is in septic shock. Her right lung has an abscess and her organs are shutting down and we don't know if she will make it. She is being transferred to Children's Hospital of the Kings Daughters in Norfolk, Virginia." It was what the media calls "flesh eating bacteria" and it was dreadfully serious.

I do not know how, but I ended up in another room. I think I passed out, but I am not sure. Maybe I just blocked out those next few minutes. The news was more than I could bear. It was more than any mother could bear. I began to question God. I remember praying at this point for the first time in years. My prayer was a plea to a god I thought was angry with me, a god who I totally misunderstood — a god who really wasn't God at all — but a counterfeit misrepresentation of the Almighty God. I prayed: *"God, I know you're mad at me. I've been so rotten, so disobedient. I know you want to take her away from me, but please don't. Please...I will dedicate her to you. I will take her to church. I will make sure she knows about you — but please don't take her from me. I know I deserve this, but please...I will dedicate her to you if you will only let me keep her."*

I distinctly remember thinking that He would be okay with me dedicating her, but that He didn't really want anything to do with me. I felt I had sinned so much that there was no hope for me. I felt I was a lost cause. I knew Stephanie was too young to be a "disappointment" to God. So, this was my plea.

Since then, I have read the story in 1 Samuel 1 about Hannah and her desperate pleas for a son. She prayed fervently for a son for many years and finally told God, "If you give me a son, I will dedicate him to you for the rest of his life". I did not realize at the time that there was a story like mine in the Bible about a desperate mother, but I will tell you that the moment I read the story for the first time, I was blown away by the comparisons. It was extremely powerful to read and is yet another example of how the Bible is so incredibly relevant in today's world.

Stephanie miraculously survived. God had plans for her. After about ten days in intensive care, she was finally well enough to go home. We were so thrilled! The day she came home, Tommy broke out with the chickenpox and I a rush of panic swept over me. He never had any complications, but I watched him closely. The next week, we heard they were coming out with a chickenpox vaccination and we were so relieved.

I began to take Stephanie to church on Sundays. I was going to hold up on my end of my bargain with God at least. Often, we would just drop her off to Sunday school and then go home to sleep off a hangover. We didn't really want to go, but I knew I had "made a deal with God" so I had to live up to my end.

It started to become apparent that Stephanie loved Jesus so much. She asked a lot of questions about Him and she had a great time going to church and memorizing Scripture. She was not playing the charade like I had done all those years ago. This was different. I think she knew in her heart that He had saved her life. All the questions she was asking made me uncomfortable because I wasn't sure how to answer them. She would look at me with wide eyes and expectation whenever she wanted to know something about Him, trusting that I would know the answer. Don't moms know everything? I would make up answers sometimes or I'd go look it up in the Bible and try to make sense of it. We eventually began to go to church more and more with her, but church was still an awkward place for me. I liked what I saw in Stephanie, but it was not my reality. "Good for her," I thought.

We moved to South Carolina when she was in second grade and joined a church there. We went more often, but we still didn't enjoy it. We just wanted what was best for our kids. Tommy seemed to really like it, too. We tried to get involved in church, but we just didn't feel the connection our kids did. I got involved anyway because I wanted to be a good example for our kids. I fell back into the familiar charade I used to play in high school, much to my dismay.

When Stephanie was in sixth grade, she was beginning to really develop a deep love for God and was feeling called into missions. She was reminding me a lot of that girl from high school – Katrina. I remember thinking back to that conversation with God in the hospital room when she was four. Had He taken me up on that? What was He doing? I wasn't sure, but I loved what my daughter was becoming. I wished down deep I could be as genuinely in love with Jesus as she was. It was truly a beautiful sight!

During this time, I was going to church and leading some Bible studies at the local YMCA. I did this because I felt like maybe God would notice and appreciate my efforts. I would think up a topic and then look it up in the concordance as preparation for each of the studies. I was beginning to want what Stephanie had more and more and I think I thought if I did all the right things, maybe God would grant it to me.

There was a woman at my church named Linda Reppert who really loved Jesus, too. She had a genuine relationship with Him and was not legalistic at all. I noted that she had the same characteristics that Katrina had in high school – people were drawn to her, she was authentic, and she did not live a life of duality. She and her best friend, Melinda, our pastor's wife, began a Bible study at my home at my request. I knew my dual life needed to end, but I wasn't sure how to break the cycle.

I had my church friends, but I also had my party friends who supported my destructive lifestyle. I was so afraid of losing my party friends if they knew I was a Christian. The song "Landslide" from Stevie Knicks expressed my feelings about them: *"I've been afraid of changing because I built my life around you…"* Inviting them to a Bible study seemed like a good idea to me. I thought if I could get them to make the decision to be Christians, too, then we could all do it together and I wouldn't have to face the possibility of losing them. My friends meant everything to me and the thought of losing them was more than I could bear. *What if they thought I was a "Jesus freak"?*

During this particular Bible study, I was pregnant with my fourth child. Our third child, Kennedy, was born a couple of years before and she was such a joy to us. Now we were expecting another precious little girl and I was getting very serious about my search for God.

I really wanted what was best for my children and somehow I knew God would be the best thing for them. But I felt something was missing. My heart was empty. It was a confusing time for me and honestly it was exhausting keeping up the charade. All the games never really changed anything, but I would always tell God I was sorry for my sins and it would make me feel better until I would wind up in the same sinful patterns again. Then I just felt defeated and like a disappointment.

When Linda and Melinda would come and share God's word with us there in my home, I was on the edge of my seat. For some reason, when they would share, it all made sense. I could tell they really loved God's Word and they lived what they were teaching us. It was not a game to them. It was their reality and I wanted it to be mine. They would answer our questions without judgment and deliver hard truths in a way that seemed very gentle and kind. I had never experienced anything like this before and it made me want to know more about God. But when I would try to read the Bible myself, I did not understand it much.

When I was pregnant, I was taking very good care of myself. When I was not pregnant, I struggled with alcohol – big time. I was drinking every day and was smoking like a chimney up until I would get pregnant. Then I would quit in an instant because I knew it was best for my child. I remember praying during my pregnancies that God would help me not to drink again. I liked how healthy I felt when I would not drink, but I hated that gnawing regret that would eat away at me when I was sober. When I would drink, I would feel numb to the emotional pain I felt. I believed that alcohol made it easier to cope with the realities of life and I was not willing to give it up – not even for God. Unfortunately, after I gave birth to my youngest daughter, Peyton, in August of 2000, I began to drink again. The shame was taking its toll on my heart.

I want to pause here, and in the best way I know how, I want to explain to you that I am not trying to say that consuming alcohol is always a sin and that God did not love me because I was a heavy drinker. I know now that God deeply and steadfastly loved me in spite of my behavior. But in my heart, I knew I had a problem with drinking. I could not imagine my life without it. It was my passion. I woke up every day, waiting and counting down until I could have the next drink. Am I saying that drinking alcohol is a sin? Well, what I am saying is that it was a sin *for me*. In Romans 14:23, the Apostle Paul reminds us to follow our convictions because if we do anything we believe is not right, we are sinning. I believe it was wrong to drink alcohol for me. The reason I know that is because it was my "god." It was my obsession. It was all I thought about and it was consuming me. Anything that takes the place of God in our hearts is an idol and I was definitely being seduced by the intoxication of alcohol.

It is not always alcohol that is responsible for the seduction in a person's life, though. Sometimes it is a toxic relationship that we know is bringing us down and keeping us from being all that God wants us to be. Sometimes it is pornography or sexual sin that we feel we cannot live without. Occasionally it is a lifestyle that we cannot imagine giving up but we know it is against God's best for us – like homosexuality or living with someone we are not married to yet. Whatever it is that we are wrestling with, the seduction is fierce and it keeps us from giving ourselves completely to God because it has convinced us that life without it will be empty and not worth living. Or maybe we feel like God is being unreasonable in his "rules". What we completely miss is that God created us and knows what is best for us and His "rules" are only there because He loves us and He does not want us living empty lives filled with pain. He is trying to protect us, not punish us. Oh, if we could grasp this reality, how different our lives would be.

Worshipping this "god" in our life can lead to pretense and living a double life because we figure if we cannot live the life we want to live down deep in our core, we can at least pretend to live that life so that others will see us as the person we desperately want to be but feel it is not possible. Our focus is not on Christ and what He has done for us – it is on our sin and failures. This is always a set up for disappointment and discouragement. We live in shame and in denial rather than in the freedom of knowing that God desperately loves us. He hates our sin, but His love for us is like that of the Father in the story in Luke chapter 15 where the son leaves the home, takes his inheritance and goes off partying and living his life for himself. When he finally returns, the Father is overjoyed and runs to him, embracing him and not angry with him. He throws a party and he celebrates that his son has finally come to his senses.

I distinctly recall about a year after Peyton was born, I had just put the kids to bed and I was sitting in my garage, drinking a beer and smoking a cigarette. I knew it was wrong but had no self-control to stop. I could almost hear an audible voice speak to me and say, "Leslie, I have so much more for you than this." I knew it was God. His voice was not condemning me as much as it was breaking my heart. I did not want to disappoint Him anymore but I felt like it was hopeless. I wished He would just leave me alone! What did He want from me anyway? I began to drink more than ever at this point and I knew in my heart that it was out of control.

Rod was in the same cycle and at this point we were co-dependent with alcohol. He would come home from work with a twelve-pack of beer that we would finish off easily each night. I always justified in my mind that since I didn't drink until after 4:00 pm that I was not an alcoholic. I mean, after all, didn't alcoholics drink from the moment they woke up? I would resist until the late afternoon, at least. I also remember thinking that since I was functioning and still able to do my duties as a mom that I must be ok. But I never thought I would be able to live without alcohol. I didn't even want to. It was as if it lied to me, convincing me that I couldn't live without it. The moment alcohol would hit my lips, all seemed well with the world. The moment the buzz would wear off or I'd wake up the next day, the reality of my double life was more than I could bear. It is what I refer to as *The Christian Charade* and, unfortunately, as I share my testimony throughout the world, I am sadly finding that it is quite prevalent in the church.

Have you ever lived a double life like I did? Maybe you are realizing at this moment that is exactly what you are doing right now. It is exhausting. I get that. I tried so hard to be a good person, make good decisions, and go to church, but in my heart I knew that was not who I was in reality. I lived in constant dread of the day my "church friends" may meet up with my "party friends" and everyone would know the truth: *I am a fraud.* I had no respect for myself and others didn't respect me either, because I would say one thing and do another.

The worst part for me, though, was that I knew God was not falling for my game. He saw right through me but He never stopped loving me and pursuing my heart anyway. Even in my sin, deception and unfaithfulness, His love never gave up on me. He wanted to change my heart and its sorry condition. He wanted to demonstrate His amazing grace to me, in spite of my sin. There was nothing I could do to make Him love me more and there was nothing I could do to make Him love me less! His love was beginning to break through my hard heart.

I was not aware of what was going on behind the scenes in my life. I did not know God had a plan that would unfold which would rock my world, bring me to my knees, and open my heart to the truth of what it means to really know Him, really love Him, and really follow Him. But soon, I would be face to face with Truth, Himself. And the condition of my heart would never be the same again.

Chapter Six

A New Heart

And so the Lord says, "These people say they are mine. They honor me with their lips, but their hearts are far from me. And their worship of me is nothing but man-made rules learned by rote." - Isaiah 29:13

February 21, 2003. I remember it vividly. It was the night my stony, stubborn heart was removed and my tender, responsive heart was transplanted. Little did I know that my life was about to change for eternity. It was a clear, chilly evening and I recall the stars were very bright against the backdrop of the velvety, black sky. My husband and I were on our way to a Discipleship Class we were required to attend in order to become members of the new church we were going to every Sunday. I was frustrated and I remember saying to Rod, "I don't know why we have to go to this class - we already know everything he's going to talk about!" He agreed, but we both went anyway because we felt we were in the right church for our family and something inside of us told us we were supposed to join. It just felt like the right thing to do.

We were sitting in the large church sanctuary, which seemed even larger because there were only about twenty-five other people there. The Pastor opened up the evening in prayer and then began to share with us what they believed as a church about who Jesus Christ is and what it means to be a Christian. As we sat there, I began to pray that my husband would really listen and understand the message that the pastor was giving about the Gospel of Jesus Christ.

I believed Jesus was the Son of God, that He died for our sins and that He rose again three days later, and since John 3:16 says, "For God so loved the world that He gave His one and only Son that whoever believes in Him will not perish, but have eternal life," I felt I was okay because I believed all that. But I wasn't so sure about my husband. He had told me a few months prior to this that he did not want to go to church on Sundays anymore after being out all night partying on Saturday night. He was either going to be a Christian 100% or he was going to hell with both guns blazing, but he was not going to be a hypocrite. Since then, I had not seen him living like a Christian at all so my fear was that he was going to hell with both guns blazing. I have always appreciated my husband's integrity so much. He has always been a man of his word and games are not something he will tolerate.

The pastor talked about things I had never, ever heard before, though. Or maybe I had heard them, but I was not listening - until this night. He described what it means to truly believe in Jesus - not just with your head (he pointed out that even

Satan believes Jesus is God's Son) but also with your *heart*. I had never heard it put that way before this night. He told us that everything changes when you become a true believer: your life, your passions, everything. I realized nothing had really changed with me, except I was getting better at the charade, and that was nothing I was proud of at all. My passions were still pretty much all about me and what made me happy, not about God and what He might want for me. I had periods of time in my life where I would get excited about Him, but those times would never last. I always ended up right back where I started. My life was not consistent with a true, heart-changing belief in Jesus that the pastor was describing.

I had said a prayer – many times, in fact, just to be sure – and even went forward and stood up to go to the front of the church, as tradition required, to ask Jesus into my heart. But I was quickly learning that my motivations had been in the wrong place. For years I put my faith in that prayer I said to keep me safe from hell, rather than putting my faith in Jesus and what He had done for me. To me, salvation was about "getting out of hell free" and I was told if I would say the prayer to receive Christ and if I believed in Jesus, I would escape hell. *I could go to heaven, but live like hell!* It seemed like the perfect solution for my self-centered life. I was so decieved. It's sad to recall those times, honestly.

As I really listened to the pastor, I realized I had been way off. I had never repented of my sin, I had never felt truly sorry for all the wrong I had done in my life. I would say I was sorry, but I knew in my heart that I had no intention of turning away from the sin. I knew it was only a matter of time before I continued in the same habits. I even recall praying for forgiveness before I would do something wrong sometimes. Pre-apologies, I suppose you could say. But true repentance is not about just saying, "I'm sorry" as much as it is about saying, "I'm through!" I had never seen a consistent change in my life. Usually when I would be sorry for what I did, it was because I had been caught, not because it was wrong and against God's best for me. I just wanted my life on my terms and did not want to submit to God's plan for my life.

At that moment, my heart felt like it was literally breaking and I was beginning to feel that same feeling I had felt in my garage that night when I was drinking a beer and smoking and I thought I heard God's voice. Just like that time in my garage, I did not feel condemned - I felt so incredibly loved. I felt His love so much this time that it was beginning to change my heart toward Him. I did not want to disappoint God anymore, but this time, as opposed to that night in the garage, I felt there was hope. I desperately wanted Him in my life. I did not care what it took or what He would ask me to give up. Nothing else mattered but that my heart was longing for God and I was finished with my double life. I was ready to give Him everything and I really meant it this time. I was through with the charade and my changing heart was beginning to pound out of my chest as tears fell down my face into my lap. I began to realize that those changes in my life that I knew in my heart I could never do were not my job anyway. They were totally God's job. My only responsibility in the process was *my* response to *His* ability in my heart.

I was beginning to realize that His love for me never quit. He was not angry with me – He had taken His anger for my sin out on Jesus Christ on the cross on Calvary over two thousand years ago. He opened my eyes, ears, and heart to the truth of what it means to truly surrender my life to Him that night. While I had prayed for my husband to see the truth, I realized I was being shown the Truth. It was overwhelming.

I was finally beginning to understand why Jesus was so important. Maybe you are reading this and wondering why Jesus did what He did and why it matters to you? I am not going to assume that just because you may have gone to church that you truly understand the Gospel because I know I was in and out of church, living the Christian charade, for twenty-three years and never understood what it meant until this night.

Romans 3:23 says that we all have sinned and fallen short of the glory of God. In Romans 5:12-21, the Apostle Paul shows us how sin began when Adam and Eve sinned in the Garden of Eden. He expresses to us that just as sin entered the world through one man (Adam), righteousness enters through one man (Jesus). Our sin separates us from a Holy God. Even if the only sin you ever commit in your life is having a bad thought, that is more sin than our Holy God will tolerate. Throughout the Old Testament, God required Sin Offerings, which were animal blood sacrifices to temporarily atone for the sins of people, but He promised throughout the Old Testament Scriptures through Prophets that a Messiah was coming and He would be the Ultimate Sacrifice for our sin. Once He came and sacrificed Himself, there would be no need for any more sacrifices. He called this the New Covenant (Hebrews 7:15-28).

Jesus is, as I tell my children, God with "skin on"! He was 100% man and 100% God (Colossians 1:15-20). He came to earth to live as a man, suffer through temptations, and all the human experiences we go through, and He did this without sinning. He showed us how to live, He showed us how to love, and He showed us how to die with integrity. I love that He did this for us. I love that He realized we could not do it without Him and instead of condemning us, He came to show us the way. It reminds me of the times I tell my kids to go clean their rooms that have become disaster areas and they just stare at me like, "How in the world am I supposed to do that?" Instead of giving them a list of things they need to do, I go into the room and walk them through it, showing them, step by step how to do it correctly. They learn much better this way. And so do we!

As a result of Jesus' sinless, perfect life, He was the only acceptable sacrifice on our behalf to God. Jesus took our sin upon Himself when He was crucified because He knew we would never be able, in our own power, to find justification with God any other way. Then He rose again three days later, defeating death and Hell, that punishment for our sins, and giving us all victory if we truly believe in Him and what He did for us.

When we put our faith and trust in Jesus alone for our righteousness, we are no longer separated from God anymore (Romans 3:22). When we believe with our heart and confess with our mouth that Jesus is Lord, we are saved from an eternity separated from God (Romans 10:9-13).

Before I continue, I want to make it clear what *believe* and *Lord* really mean. The New Testament was originally written in the Greek language and as the books and letters have been translated into English, the meaning can sometimes come off as pretty shallow, in my opinion. The original Greek word that we have translated as believe is *pisteuo* and it actually means a firm conviction and a full surrender. Your lifestyle will begin to reflect this conviction and belief. The original Greek word that we have translated as "Lord" in Romans 10:9 was *kyrios* and it means the owner, one who has control of the person, the master. So, the question we ask ourselves is really, "Do I have a firm conviction, a full surrender and a lifestyle that reflects the fact that Jesus is in control of my life, that He is my Master?"

It is not about our behavior, our "trying" to do the right thing. God accepts us just as we are — sinners in need of grace — and He is the one who makes us right in His eyes by forgiving our sins and giving us His Spirit to help us live out our life here on earth. Ezekiel 36:27 reminds us, *"And I will put my Spirit within you so that you will follow my decrees and be careful to obey my regulations."* Without His Spirit, we are trying so hard to make ourselves right, but we cannot, in our own efforts, ever do enough "right" things to justify ourselves in the sight of God. I suppose you could say it's not a matter of *trying* as much as it is about *dying* — dying to ourselves and our old passions and desires. We begin to trust that God will give us new desires and a new life — which He clearly says He will do when we give Him our lives (2 Corinthians 5:17). Salvation is a free gift from God — but it costs us our life. By giving up our lives for God, trusting Him and accepting Him as Lord, we are finally able to experience what it means to truly live an authentic and wholehearted life. This is the spiritual heart transplant.

The issue I had faced for so long was that I was not willing to put my trust and faith in Jesus alone. I was putting my faith in myself, in my works, in a prayer, and in the fact that I believed the story about Jesus. I was trying to impress God with all I was doing on the outside, but was unwilling to allow Him access to the inside – my heart. He wanted to give me a new heart, one that beat for Him, but I had been holding onto my old heart and put my trust in my desires and myself. But this night at this Discipleship Class, I realized that I was finished and I knew beyond a shadow of a doubt that whatever it took, whatever He would ask of me, I would do it because I was beginning to see how much He loved me. He gave His life for me. His sacrifice was all I needed.

At the end of the Discipleship Class, the pastor asked those of us who wanted to give their lives to Christ to raise our hands while everyone's eyes were closed. He walked us through a prayer to receive Christ but this prayer was so different than the many other times I had prayed it in my life. I had already decided prior to this prayer that I was giving God everything, and I felt this was just like the formal commitment I was making in my heart to Him.

I suppose you could compare it to the wedding ceremony. The bride and groom know what is going to happen at the ceremony. They have already committed themselves to one another through words, recognize their love for one another, and they joyfully anticipate being able to declare their vows to one another as they solidify their commitment to share their lives together. That's what it felt like to me this time. The other times I said this prayer, my motivation was selfish and about what I could get from God and how I could stay out of hell. This time I was declaring my vows to my precious Savior! I was making a real commitment to Him. I was incredibly sorry for my sin and this prayer was more about how thankful I was for the forgiveness He was offering me through His Son, Jesus. I was so humbled that He would sacrifice so much for me and was overwhelmed that I was being given such a beautiful gift. I felt so unworthy, but so thankful. I was bursting inside!

After we finished praying, our pastor asked everyone to stand if they had prayed to accept Christ as Lord and Savior. My husband stood to his feet beside me as everyone looked on and clapped. I was so overwhelmed by God's presence and I was so shocked and thrilled at what had just happened in my own life and in my husband's life together that I had no strength to stand. My mind was whirling, my heart was pounding and my legs were weak. I had been awakened to the truth for the first time in my life. I knew I had a new heart this time. There was no question. Well, until I was on my way home.

On our drive home, Rod and I discussed the entire class and most especially what had just happened in our lives and in our hearts. But something was bothering me and it became clear that my past experiences in following the strict rules of a church were rearing their ugly head. I was concerned that my decision was not real to God because I did not physically stand at the end of the service, as the Pastor had instructed. He even used a Scripture from Matthew 10:33 where Jesus says if we stand for Him on earth, He will stand for us in heaven. But my legs just would not lift me up. Had I denied Jesus by not standing that night? I hoped not. Rod and I both agreed it did not matter, that my heart change was something new and my physical stance was not as important to God as the realization that He was changing me from the inside out.

As the days went by, I slowly began to see evidences of my new life. I was enjoying and even comprehending Scripture, I was praying more, and I felt more connected to God than ever. There were words I used to say that I just could not, in good conscience, say anymore. I was not able to watch the same television shows that I used to think were so funny. I began to find them offensive! It did not feel like a forced effort anymore with God. I would wake up in the morning and my first thought would be, "Good morning, Lord! What do you have for me today?" It was really overwhelming to be experiencing a real relationship with God. I was really enjoying getting to know my Heavenly Father intimately! The best part is — it was all coming from inside of me, not just a show on the outside.

I will be honest, though, I still had my moments of struggling with doubt. It would usually start with the thought, "You did not stand for Him, remember? You really did not change. You are still a fraud." These thoughts would usually happen when I would skip my Scripture reading or when I would choose to sin instead of doing the right thing. Remember we talked about how Jeannie takes medicine twice per day in her post-transplant care routine? This is what I consider the healing balm for our new heart — God's Word and time spent with Him. I would then pray and ask God to forgive and strengthen me and He did. Each time this happened, I would remind myself of Romans 8:1, *"There is now no condemnation for those who are in Christ Jesus."* My salvation was not based on anything I could do anyway - it was all based on Him and what He did! I just needed to trust Him.

My husband and I decided to get baptized a couple of weeks after the Discipleship Class, as an act of obedience to God and a public declaration of our new lives in Christ. We invited several of our "party friends" to attend the ceremony, the friends who we loved so much and were so afraid of losing if we gave our lives completely to God. They were so kind to show up and witness our baptism. I so desperately wanted them to follow Jesus, too, but I felt I had been a bad example over the years of living a double life and claiming to be a Christian but living contrary to what I said I believed. I knew this time was different though and I knew I would probably lose some of my old friends, but I trusted God and knew that He would give me new friends that would encourage me to live my Christian life in obedience and with integrity. But I was not going to give them up without a fight and I felt having them there was my last ditch effort to prove to them that this time, it was different. I really had changed. This time *God* was changing me.

Up to this point, Rod and I were still drinking occasionally but were not getting drunk anymore. We were slightly convicted, but found our desire to grow closer to God was beginning to edge out our desire for alcohol. I had a wise friend tell me that I needed to stop focusing so much on my sin and instead focus on my relationship with God – He would take care of the rest. I realized that if God wanted me to stop drinking, He would convict my heart and my life would change, but I could not force it. It had to come from Him.

As the pastor lowered me into the baptismal water in front of the packed church, I was praying and thanking God for giving me an opportunity to proclaim publically what He was doing inside of me personally. I felt Him whisper to my heart as I rose up out of the water, "The water represents alcohol in your life. Rise up and walk into your new life. You are free!"

I honestly do not know how else to explain it but to tell you it was a heart whisper I heard that day. I knew He healed me at that moment and I knew He did not want me to drink alcohol anymore. Alcohol had been my god for far too long and He was ready to show me a better way. I was walking out of the bondage of alcoholism and into my new life. It felt like a tender embrace from God as they draped the fluffy, warm towels over my shoulders and dried me off beside the baptismal in the dark corner of the church. I would never be the same after this night and I knew it.

A week later, we were invited to a birthday party for a friend who was in attendance at our baptism. Rod and I were facing a strong temptation to drink alcohol. We both succumbed to the alcohol and drank far too much that night. I awoke the next morning with gnawing conviction (and a nasty hangover) that left me overwhelmed and deeply sorry. My first instinct was to run and hide, like what I had read in Genesis when Adam and Eve sinned in the Garden of Eden. I was so ashamed of myself and I didn't want to disappoint God – again. I even thought He probably wished He had never given me that second chance since I blew it. But instead of running from God, I prayed and asked Him to forgive me.

I read Psalm 51, the Psalm that King David wrote after he sinned by committing adultery and murder. He didn't run from God. Instead, he ran *to* God and he confessed he was wrong, he wrote one of the most beautiful prayers of restoration I have ever read. I thought since he was known as a man after God's own heart, he might be someone I would want to emulate. My new, tender and responsive heart was showing me the correct way to repent and to confess my sin to God and it was much sweeter than the guilt, condemnation and regret I used to experience! I prayed that prayer that morning and God overwhelmingly answered it.

[1] Have mercy on me, O God,
because of your unfailing love.
Because of your great compassion,
blot out the stain of my sins.
[2] Wash me clean from my guilt.
Purify me from my sin.
[3] For I recognize my rebellion;
it haunts me day and night.
[4] Against you, and you alone, have I sinned;
I have done what is evil in your sight.
You will be proved right in what you say,
and your judgment against me is just.
[5] For I was born a sinner—
yes, from the moment my mother conceived me.
[6] But you desire honesty from the womb,
teaching me wisdom even there.
[7] Purify me from my sins, and I will be clean;
wash me, and I will be whiter than snow.
[8] Oh, give me back my joy again;
you have broken me—
now let me rejoice.
[9] Don't keep looking at my sins.
Remove the stain of my guilt.
[10] Create in me a clean heart, O God.
Renew a loyal spirit within me.
[11] Do not banish me from your presence,
and don't take your Holy Spirit from me.

¹² Restore to me the joy of your salvation,
and make me willing to obey you.
¹³ Then I will teach your ways to rebels,
and they will return to you.
¹⁴ Forgive me for shedding blood, O God who saves;
then I will joyfully sing of your forgiveness.
¹⁵ Unseal my lips, O Lord,
that my mouth may praise you.
¹⁶ You do not desire a sacrifice, or I would offer one.
You do not want a burnt offering.
¹⁷ The sacrifice you desire is a broken spirit.
You will not reject a broken and repentant heart, O God.
—*Psalm 51:1-17 (NLT)*

All day long, I noticed Rod and I were avoiding each other. God had been working on his new heart all day, too. We finally locked eyes around three o'clock in the afternoon and wept as we held one another and said, "Never again. God does not want this for us. We are done with alcohol." We poured every drop of alcohol we had in our home down the drain. That was March 21, 2003. We have not, by God's grace alone, had a single drop since that night. He healed us. He took our passion for alcohol away and gave us a new passion and it was *Him!*

As the years went by, Rod and I grew so much in our faith. It hasn't always been easy, that's for sure. No matter the circumstances, however, we always knew God was there, guiding us, cheering us on, and as we read His Word and prayed we learned to really trust Him. I began working in Christian radio as a Morning Show Co-Host at a station in Charlotte, North Carolina in April of 2004, a little over a year after my spiritual heart transplant. I loved my job and God gave me such a passion to share my life over the airwaves with the listeners, whom I loved deeply.

A little over three years later, I found myself competing as a contestant on an internationally televised reality show. I auditioned for this show for many years and Rod and I were in agreement that even if I was never selected as a contestant, it was something I was to continue to pursue. The goal was never to get on the show as much as it was to be obedient to what we believed God was asking me to do. After eleven auditions, I was finally selected to be on the show. I had complete faith that God had a plan in all of this, but somehow I knew it was never about the money, which was a million dollar prize. I knew my reason for going had to be so much more than that.

What I did not realize at the time was that God was going to use my time on that show to not only impact my heart, but also the hearts of millions of people watching, worldwide.

Chapter Seven

Heart Examination

*Examine yourselves to see if your faith is genuine. Test
yourselves. Surely you know that Jesus Christ is among
you; if not, you have failed the test of genuine faith.*
-2 Corinthians 13:5

In the first episode of the competition, all of the contestants
were ushered into a "welcoming ceremony" in the country of
China. This ceremony took place in a Buddhist temple. When
told to bow before the huge Buddha as part of this "welcoming
ceremony," I excused myself and left the temple. When the
show's host asked me why I would not participate nor remain
in the temple, I said, "I'm not religious, but I have a relationship
with Jesus Christ and I'm only going to put my face on the
floor for Him." I did not last long on the show – just three
episodes. It was heartbreaking to be "voted out" by my fellow
contestants. They would later tell me it was because I was too
nice for the game – they did not think I would play the kind

of game that they were going to play in order to win, so they had to get rid of me. I suppose that works for me! But I had a producer, who just happened to be a Jewish man, contact me online and say, "Leslie, I know you're disappointed you didn't last longer on the show. But I want you to know that you had more of an impact in nine days than most people do in an entire season. You should be very proud."

God, by His amazing grace, gave me another opportunity to stand for Him and this time, He gave me the strength to do it in front of over fifteen million people. I am so grateful. Not only did He give me this gift, but also He has used this public stance to open doors of opportunity for me to share my faith with the other contestants, the show's producers and staff, and people all over the world. I no longer beat myself up about "not standing" that night at the Discipleship Class because in my heart, I know God is whispering, *"Leslie, you may not have stood physically that night at church, but for the first time in your life, you stood for me in your heart."*

All those years of standing and going forward to the church altar physically and praying a prayer to keep me out of hell did nothing on the inside of me. It was only when I stood in my heart that it truly counted. God did not want my empty promises. He did not even want me to change my life. He just wanted my heart and I finally gave it to Him. Then when He asked me to stand physically, I did, and it was not out of duty, fear, or rules. It was because I loved Him and wanted to stand for Him.

There was a church I used to go to called *Transformation Church* in Fort Mill, South Carolina. Something we would repeat after every service was, "Upward, Inward, Outward!" This showed that if we look upward and focus on our relationship with God first and foremost, we will have an inward change as we are taught to love Jesus, love ourselves correctly and love others compassionately. Once we do this, there will be an outward change that comes from an overflow of what is going on inside, in the heart of who we really are. That is how God changes us from the inside out, and only He can do this.

If you've stood for Jesus outwardly many times, but inside you are not sure where your heart stands, you could be deceived just as I was for so many years. I consider this deception the cruelest deception of all. I believe it is why Jesus used these words in Matthew 7:21-23: *"Not everyone who says to me, 'Lord, Lord', will enter the kingdom of heaven, but only he who does the will of my Father who is in heaven. Many will say to me on that day, 'Lord, Lord, did we not prophesy in your name, and in your name drive out demons and perform many miracles?' Then I will tell them plainly, 'I never knew you. Away from me, you evildoers!'"*

My friend, these are people in the church who are being addressed by Jesus. I cannot think of any other group of people in the world who are doing things in Jesus' name. These are people who are playing the game. People who are deeply deceived. These "many" people are focused on how things look on the outside and not on the inside changes in the heart where God is searching. These are people whose heads are full of knowledge and pride, but whose hearts are empty of faith and true (*pisteuo)* belief.

Was I "saved" when I was ten years old? A lot of people ask me this. My answer is this: Christ took my sins upon Himself on Calvary over two thousand years ago. When I was ten, I began the process of discovering who He is and why I needed to know Him. And when I was thirty-three years old, I finally accepted His gift and was given a new heart – a spiritual heart transplant. Is it possible I was deceived during those twenty-three years in the church? Yes, I believe it is possible. But here is what I do not want you to miss: *God pursued me.* God didn't give up on me. God never stopped loving me! He knew before the world began that I was going to follow Him and accept His forgiveness. That's all that matters. And I *know* beyond a shadow of a doubt that I am a true believer now.

I pray you will get honest with yourself and with God. He loves you so much. He, and only He, knows your heart and your intentions. I encourage you to take a look at your life since that moment when you asked Him into your heart. I am not saying that your works will save you, so I am not asking you to look at your good works as proof of your salvation. What I am asking is more about your inward changes. Did you truly repent of your sins? Repenting does not just mean, "I'm sorry," it means, "I'm through!" What I used to do was tell God how sorry I was for my sin, but then I'd go and do it all over again. I felt like if I just asked forgiveness I would be fine and I could continue to live however I wanted. I was wrong and I see that clearly now.

Do you live a double life? This is a red flag that your decision may not have been from your heart. I know how wrong in my heart that it felt to be two different people, but I did not realize I had an option! If I were honest, I'd admit I thought everyone at church was doing that exact same thing because when I looked around, I witnessed many people just like me who were living on both sides of the fence. I also noticed those who were not. These were the people who really stood out to me because when I saw their genuine faith being walked out, I could not deny that it was possible to be an authentic believer who did not play the charade. They were not perfect, but they were authentic. I wanted to be that kind of person so badly, but I did not know how.

Is there a change in your life? Not the self-induced kind that wears you out, but the kind that comes from deep within. Please hear me and hear me loud and clear: I am *not* promoting a works-based salvation. In other words, I'm not saying there is anything more that you need to do except believe in your heart (*pisteuo* - firm conviction, full surrender) that Jesus is who He says He is and confess with your mouth that Jesus is Lord (*kyrios* -the owner; one who has control of the person, the master). Repentance is not a work that you do, it is a supernatural conviction where you realize you are going in the wrong direction, and so you turn toward Jesus. Salvation is not about what you do — it's about what He did because He knew you could never do enough! When you have truly given your life to Jesus, you begin to do things with a new motive because you are given a new heart. This motive is love, appreciation and compassion that overflow from a changed heart. Religion produces changes that are outward and done out of fear, obligation and because you think you will "look good" to others or even to God.

You cannot help but change when the Holy Spirit gets a hold of you. It is slow sometimes, but there is always a change — even if it is small. There are always signs of life when a heart begins to beat! A true believer realizes all that Christ has done for her and she wants to change out of a heart of gratitude, not obligation. A true believer will still sin, but will feel genuine, godly sorrow over her sin and will repent (turn away from and ask forgiveness). When I speak to audiences, I always say, "I double-dog dare you to try to continue in habitual sin if you are a true believer in Jesus! If you do, you will be absolutely miserable. The conviction in your heart will be overwhelming. You will not be able to keep it up." Yes, you can live in habitual sin as a believer for weeks, months or even years – but you will be so miserable because your relationship with Jesus will be strained. It's a matter of time before your broken heart over your sin will win. That is such an incredible hope that we have as believers.

Do you desire to know God more intimately, to have Him as more than just a "get out of hell free card"? This is another symptom of a God-changed heart. You long for a real relationship with Him. You pray, you read His word with joy, and it begins to really become a huge part of your life as you realize it is a personal love letter written from God straight to you. Yes, hell is a devastating reality. People who do not receive a new heart from Him will spend eternity there, the Bible is very clear about this. But if getting out of hell is the only reason you want to be "saved", please ask yourself this question: If Jesus were not in heaven, would you still want to go there? A changed heart will have a deep and abiding love for Him. Your heart will overflow with thanks for what He has done for you.

One indication that I knew God had truly changed my heart was when I began to really understand the Scriptures in a new and deeper way. All of a sudden, the verses from the Bible that I memorized as a child dropped from my head into my new heart and burst forth with life in a way that is almost hard for me to explain. They made sense now! I will allow the Apostle Paul to explain this from his letter to the Christians in the city of Corinth in ancient Greece: *"But people who aren't spiritual can't receive these truths from God's Spirit. It all sounds foolish to them and they can't understand it, for only those who are spiritual can understand what the Spirit means."* (1 Corinthians 2:14)

My view of God was warped for so many years. I did not understand His perfect love and compassion for me at all. I did not understand that He wanted a relationship with me but my sin was preventing that from happening and I never understood that He had made a way through Jesus for that relationship to be restored. All along, I thought He was angry and did not want to be anywhere near me, but now I knew better. I thought my sin was more than He was willing to forgive. I was wrong.

An illustration of this can be made in life of our new friend, Jeannie. The day after her heart transplant, her children were very eager to see her. They missed her so much. But Jeannie was very prone to infection after such a serious surgery and the doctors were insistent that if anyone in her family had an illness, they were not to go into her room because of her vulnerability to infection. Unfortunately, her youngest and her oldest children both had been fighting the flu. Her middle child was not sick, so he was able to come and sit with his mother beside her bed.

Her other two children had their faces pressed against the window of the cold hospital door and longingly watched as their mother lifted her hand and waved at them. She wanted desperately to hold them, to love them up close and to spend time with them, but their illness separated them from their beloved mother. If she only had a perfect cure that could be poured over her children that would sanitize them and cure them of their illness! Then she could embrace them, kiss their little cheeks and let them know everything was going to be okay. But this was not possible.

My friend, you and I have an illness, too. Our illness is our sin. Though Jeannie's condition made her weak and vulnerable, our Heavenly Father's holiness makes Him strong and powerful. Our sin would contaminate His holiness, so He will not allow sin near Him. But that does not change His love for us. So He made a way for us to enter through the door – and that Way is Jesus Christ. His precious, perfect blood was shed for us and covers us, instantly sanitizing and healing us of our nasty illness, sin. We now have direct access to God through Jesus Christ when we put our faith and trust in Him.

When someone does something wrong, there must be justice, or payment for that wrong that was committed. If you think of a court setting, it is as if Jesus is saying to the Judge (God), "I have her covered, Father. I paid for her sins. She is innocent!" But He cannot and will not force Himself on us. We must accept His covering by believing in Him, trusting Him and having complete faith that He alone is our Advocate – not our works, not our good deeds, not our good intentions or our empty promises. When we trust in Jesus alone, God looks at us and says, "Not guilty."

We must believe that Jesus did this for us, but believing, as we discussed earlier in this chapter, means so much more than just acknowledging something to be true. It means a firm conviction, a full surrender, and your life will reflect that surrender. It's the difference between, "Sure, I believe Rod is my husband," (Because we know he is) and "I believe in Rod so much that I would trust him with my life."

Do you believe in Jesus? I mean, really believe. Do you trust Jesus with your life? Have you given Him full access to your heart? Have you had a "spiritual heart transplant"? If so, you are not the same as you were. You stand for Him by the way you are living your life - each and every day. You will still have difficulties in your life, but you will never go through them alone again. He will never leave you and He will never turn you away.

When I think back to the way I used to take such fine care of myself when I was pregnant with my children, I cannot help but see a parallel. It wasn't about me when I was pregnant – it was about those children growing inside of me. Making right choices for myself was natural and easy when it wasn't about me. It is like that now, too. I carry Jesus around in me – not in my womb, but in my heart.

Our precious daughter that we almost lost to a devastating illness ended up being the conduit that God used to show us what a real relationship with Jesus Christ looked like. I often think about that day when I dedicated her to Him in that hospital room, assuming He wanted her, but not me. I sometimes wonder if He might have said, *"Yes, I want her. But I want you, too, my dear. She will show you the way."*

Chapter Eight

Heart Monitor

*"Guard your heart above all else, for it
determines the course of your life."*
-Proverbs 4:23

I awoke to a brand new day. My first thoughts, before my head even left my pillow, were about the night before. It was the night I surrendered my life to Jesus Christ – the night of my spiritual heart transplant. I began to wonder if it was all real this time, or if it would fade away like all of the previous vain attempts to repair my life on my own. This time seemed different though. I was not relying on my own virtue or intentions. This time, I was relying on Jesus to do it all through me and I truly believed He would.

As an exercise instructor for many years, I knew how the accountability of showing up for class had been so important in my own fitness. I liked that I had to be there because if

I did not go to class, there would not be a class! I needed the accountability that it gave to me and I knew I wanted accountability and wisdom if I was going to walk this new path of true Christianity.

In retrospect, the Holy Spirit must have instilled my desire for a mentor and accountability into my new heart. I honestly did not know at the time that what I was sensing was actually quite Biblical. In Titus, chapter 2, Paul instructs Titus on how to promote right teaching in the church. He specifically says in verse three, *"Similarly, teach the older women to live in a way that honors God. They must not slander others or be heavy drinkers. Instead, they should teach others what is good. These older women must train the younger women to love their husbands and their children, to live wisely and be pure, to work in their homes, to do good, and to be submissive to their husbands. Then they will not bring shame on the Word of God."*

The element that grabs me about this is where Paul says, "these older women *must* train the younger women." I am also struck by the last sentence: *then they will not bring shame on the Word of God.* So, it is possible to bring shame on the Word of God if, as older women in the faith, we do not train and mentor the younger women. This is not negotiable. It is clearly something God takes very seriously. I did not know this at the time, but I am so thankful He stirred my heart to pursue an experienced woman to help me walk out my new-found faith.

I prayed for a mentor. I immediately thought of my friend, Linda Reppert. She was one of those faithful women who lead that Bible study in my home a few years prior to this. After many days of prayer, I picked up the phone to call her and was shaking as I told her what had happened in my heart.

For years, Linda believed I was already a Christian. I talked the talk in front of her and even walked the walk when she was around. But there was a secret I had been hiding for a long time that I was about to share with her and I was terrified she would be angry with me for not being truthful with her. I recall praying about it before I called her, saying, "God, I am so sorry I have been lying for all of these years. Please forgive me for being a deceiver." I did not hear an audible voice but I did sense a voice echo in the depths of my heart that said, "You are not a deceiver – you have been deeply deceived." It was true – my heart had been deceived for many years. It was not as if I had played this game with full knowledge of my not really knowing Christ as Lord and Savior. I was under the assumption that Christianity was a game, not a reality! I had placed my faith in a prayer, not in what Christ had done for me. I really believed everyone lived a double life and just pretended all the time. I did not realize it was actually *possible* to truly know Jesus on an intimate level.

Linda did not react at all the way I feared she would. She was surprised, of course, but said loudly, "Praise the LORD! I'm so happy for you, Leslie! This is wonderful news." Then she prayed for me. I asked her if I could bring her lunch later that day and have a talk with her face to face. She agreed and I was there within a few hours with lunch and a huge favor to ask of her. These days, she jokes, *"I had no idea how much a free lunch would end up costing me!"*

As we had our lunch out on the deck of her home, we both shed tears of delight as we recalled the events of the night I surrendered my heart to Jesus. I told her that I knew I needed help if I was going to grow in my faith in Christ and I knew I wanted her to have a role in helping me grow. I had seen her walk it out. I respected her, and honestly, I wanted what she had! She did not agree to this right away, but told me she would pray about it. Initially, I thought, "What's to pray about? This is perfect!" but I realize, in retrospect, that it was absolutely essential that she take the time to pray and make sure it was a "God thing" and not just a "good thing" to do. Sometimes we commit to things and we do not consult the Lord, as we should.

There is an example of this in Joshua, chapter nine. The people of Gibeon heard what Joshua and his men had done in conquering many of the lands around them, so they resorted to deception to approach Joshua and his men to save themselves. They knew how strong he was and that they did not stand a prayer against the Israelites and their God. So, they made up a story and told them they were from a "distant" land and told them they needed protection. They even made it look like they came from a distant land by wearing out their clothing and showing them their stale bread that, they said, had been taken out of the oven right before their "long journey". Joshua and his men inspected the evidence and agreed to a peace treaty with these people, not knowing they were really Gibeonites. They ratified the agreement with a binding oath.

Verse 14 of Joshua nine tells us, *"So the Israelites examined their food, but they did not consult the Lord."* Three days after making the treaty, they learned that the people lived nearby. They were their enemies and yet because they had made a binding oath (something that was never broken in those days) they were stuck with protecting the very people they should have been conquering.

Moral of that story: always consult the Lord before a big decision – even when you feel strongly that it is something you should do. Mentoring is a big decision. It is a binding oath – a very important relationship. God never wants us to jump into a binding relationship like this without consulting Him first. It can lead to heartbreak and avoidable frustrations if not done in the order God instructs.

To put it in perspective, this relationship is as important in a spiritual heart transplant recipient as a heart monitor is to a heart patient. It is implanted near to the heart, not to monitor the external, but to monitor the internal workings of the heart. A mentor is someone near to our heart that helps us monitor the internal heart activity and helps keep our new heart healthy and strong, spiritually speaking. A heart monitor can tell you what is going on in the heart, but it cannot change what is going on in the heart. A mentor cannot change us, but they can help diagnose those issues that, with the help of Christ, we can change.

After a few days of prayer, Linda called me and we set up a meeting. The funny thing about Linda and my relationship is that we are so very different. I think that is what made her pause initially before committing to anything. For example, our personalities are kind of like our hair products: hers are to give her hair more body and mine are to tame my hair down. She is super organized and I am, well, let's just say I'm not. She is very detail oriented and makes lists. I lack the discipline of detail and only use lists to spit my used gum into when I am finished with it. Yes, we are different, but that's why, I believe it works so well. You do not have to be exactly alike in order for a mentoring relationship to work. God uses all types.

As I just established, Linda is a list-person, so of course she made up a list of guidelines she wanted to go over with me before she would agree to be my mentor. I listened intently as she explained each idea, one by one. I want to share this list with you (I think my mentor is rubbing off on me) because I think the guidelines she came up with are not only Biblical, but are very important as you begin a mentoring-type relationship with someone. Here is the list:

1. She told me we would both commit to this for just one year. Sometimes in the relationship, you may realize it is not working out well for both people involved. If that is the case, there is a one-year commitment that is in place from the get-go where you can go over the first year and see if you are feeling led to continue. It's been ten years since that commitment was made between Linda and me and we are still going strong! But knowing that we had an "out" (if need be) was very helpful as we learned about one another more and grew in our relationship. If we had parted ways, we would not have taken it so personally since we knew it was only a year's commitment from the beginning.

2. She told me to be in the Word of God myself, not to just rely on her to keep me "plugged into God". I am so glad she told me to do this. I know it seems like a no-brainer, but it really is easy to live vicariously through someone else, spiritually speaking. I truly believe my commitment to read, study and meditate on God's word on my own was a big reason I grew so much in the first year of my walk with God! I shared what I would learn with her and she would give me feedback,

pray with me and help me to dig deeper by encouraging me. She never gave me answers – she just prayed for me and pointed me to the One who could. Every good mentor works that way – pointing the mentee to Jesus, Himself.

3. She told me that she needed permission to point out any sin she might see in my life (and gave me permission to do the same to her). This would be a relationship built on trust and communication. This has happened a few times throughout our time together and I can honestly say I have never been angry with her once for doing it because she does it with such grace, love and with a desire to see me restored, not a desire to "be right" or make me feel bad. Loving correction is essential in a mentoring relationship – and this takes time and trust to build.

4. She told me she was going to hold me accountable about remaining humble. Especially as I grew as a public speaker, radio personality and reality show contestant, she called me out a few times. It is so important to surround yourself with people who love you and want to encourage your relationship with God, even if it means pointing out the hard stuff. She is used by God to remind me that I am merely a vessel with the incredible privilege of sharing with others the Treasure I hold inside.

Once we discussed these four guidelines, we prayed and began our new mentoring relationship. It has truly been a blessing for me and I feel that Linda has become my "spiritual mama". Since then, I have started to mentor some young women, myself. I have learned so much about what to do and what not to do through her example.

Our new heart is vulnerable, my friend. The enemy of your soul knows he cannot have you anymore because once you belong to Jesus, He holds you forever. But now Satan's new mission is to render you useless. He heaps condemnation on you when you mess up. He tempts you to isolate yourself when you are going through a difficult time. Having someone walk beside you who has already been down this road is so reassuring.

As I said before, mentors and friends who you share your faith and struggles with remind me of heart monitors. There are actually three types of heart monitors available:

1. There is a 24-hour heart monitor that you wear on the outside of your body with patches attached to you to record the activity of your heart. This monitor would be like a friend you would meet for coffee or lunch occasionally in order to sharpen you, challenge you, pray with you and enjoy the her company.

2. There is a 21-day monitor that is similar to the one above in design, but you wear it for three weeks instead of 24-hours. This monitor is similar to a close friend you are in a relationship with whom you share more of what is going on in your heart in regular intervals. She is a closer friend whom you can confide in about the things you are really struggling with in your life.

3. The heart implant monitor is actually implanted under the skin – very close to the heart. This monitors the heart 24/7 until it is removed, typically one to three years. This is the one

that is like a mentoring relationship. You get beyond the surface of what is going on and there is a commitment to share with this person for a longer period of time.

Linda is like the third example for me. God has implanted her next to my heart and she has been used greatly by Him in my life to help me grow and learn in my faith. I trust her and I know she always has my best interest in mind. I know she is in the Word of God and I see her walking it out. She is not perfect, but she is honest and she is the older woman God has brought into my life to help me be the best I can be.

Maybe you are thinking right now, "This all sounds great, but I do not know anyone who I could ask to be my mentor." I have heard this a lot of times. I highly suggest that you begin praying right now for the Lord to direct you to the person He has for you. I urge you to keep your eyes and ears open to His leading. If He puts this desire in your heart, He will lead you to the right mentor. We already read in Titus 2 that mentoring is something He desires for us, so why wouldn't He provide someone for us?

If you are older in the faith, please pray about being a mentor to someone younger in the faith. You do not have to have it all together, you do not have to be super-spiritual and you do not have to know all the answers. You just have to be willing to allow God to lead you; humble enough to admit you cannot do this without Him and trusting enough to have faith that He will use you...*because He will.*

Chapter Nine

A Religious Heart

*"What sorrow awaits you teachers of religious law and you Pharisees.
Hypocrites! For you are like whitewashed tombs—beautiful on the
outside but filled on the inside with dead people's bones and all
sorts of impurity. Outwardly you look like righteous people, but
inwardly your hearts are filled with hypocrisy and lawlessness."
Matthew 23:27-28*

I do not know what got into us on that hot, California summer
day in 1980, but my sister and I were up to no good. Mom
was working in the church office and we had to wait on her to
get some things done so we wandered around on the church
property (this was the church I spoke to you about in the
beginning of the book– the one that was focused heavily on
"behavior modification" but not so much on grace). We found
some wild gourds growing on the side of the church and decided
it would be fun to throw about twelve of them, smashing them

into pieces all over the parking lot. It felt naughty and wrong, but I could not help myself.

The pastor was very angry with us when he realized what we had done. In fact, he was so angry that he took us into the office and had us paddled. He said those gourds were his "personal gourds" and he was growing them for a purpose. Granted, I believe we needed to be disciplined because what we did was absolutely wrong. But there is much more to this whole story than meets the eye.

This church was, if you recall, very controlling of our family. Word got out about our "rebellious" and "unruly" ways and we were frowned upon, talked about and our parents were absolutely humiliated. It was as if we had to earn our way back into the "inside circle". Until we proved we were worthy, we were the outcasts and my parents paid the highest price. We would have been fine if the discipline stopped at the paddling, but it went on and on through the glances, judgment and cruelty displayed toward us by the very people we considered our church family.

Down deep in my heart, I think I may have been as bitter toward my step-father as those gourds probably tasted because he allowed us to go to this controlling and legalistic church for so long. I carried resentment around in my heart for many years. But after reading 2 Kings 4, I feel differently about the whole situation.

In 2 Kings 4, verses 38-41, I read this:

Elisha now returned to Gilgal, and there was a famine in the land. One day as the group of prophets was seated before him, he said to his servant, "Put a large pot on the fire, and make some stew for the rest of the group."

One of the young men went out into the field to gather herbs and came back with a pocketful of wild gourds. He shredded them and put them into the pot without realizing they were poisonous. Some of the stew was served to the men. But after they had eaten a bite or two they cried out, "Man of God, there's poison in this stew!" So they would not eat it.

Elisha said, "Bring me some flour." Then he threw it into the pot and said, "Now it's all right; go ahead and eat." And then it did not harm them.

As I read this during the wee morning hours about two years ago, my "smashing gourds" act came to mind. When that happened, I knew God wanted to teach me something important, so I prayed for wisdom and understanding. I realized quickly that the servant of Elisha was really trying to do a good thing – and so was my step-father. The servant did not realize the gourds were poisonous; he was just trying to feed the people. My step-father was doing the same – trying to feed his family, spiritually speaking. He did not know much about God or the Bible and he wanted us to learn and grow. He really meant well, he was just misled. I could not blame him for that. I immediately released the resentment that I held onto for so long and my heart began to change.

The gourds, to me, represent the legalism and man-made religion that can seep in and poison the church. Legalism is when we strive to do things in order to please God. It is a rule-based mentality and it can destroy our relationship with God because we begin to weigh the good versus the bad in our lives and we begin to believe the lie that God accepts us based on our performance instead of what Christ did for us on the Cross.

What was Elisha's solution in 2 Kings 4? He sprinkled flour into the pot of stew. What on earth could that possibly mean? In researching the original text of the scripture, the word "flour" was actually the Hebrew word *quemach,* which is the word for "meal". It was the flour used to make bread. And who is the Bread of Life, according to John 6:35? Jesus Christ. So when Elisha sprinkled flour into the stew, God could be showing us that when we sprinkle the Truth – Jesus – into our poisonous stew of legalism and man-made religion, He will make it healthy and nourishing. What a miracle!

Bitterness had entered my heart as I thought about how I was exposed to legalism, but now I have a completely different perspective. Though I was raised for a few years in this false teaching, I can also say that I was raised in the Scriptures. God's Word does not return without accomplishing what it was sent out to do, according to Isaiah 55:11. All of the scriptures that I memorized during those years at a legalistic church have come to life inside of my heart now that I have found a true relationship with Jesus. What a blessing that has been in my life. Though they were just mere words to me then, they are life-giving words that are imbedded in my heart now and for that I am so grateful.

If you have been raised in the poisonous stew of bitter-gourd legalism, just sprinkle the truth of Jesus into your stew and watch what He does. He takes what the enemy meant for harm in your life and miraculously changes your poisonous stew into a nutritious and healthy meal if you will allow Him.

By the way, it is not lost on me that I was smashing those bitter-tasting gourds on the road as a young girl. I feel it was a sneak peek into my future. God was graciously showing me I would be smashing those poisonous things as part of my ministry for many years down the road. Which brings me to the point of this chapter and possibly this entire book.

Our striving must cease if we are going to be able to walk in the freedom Christ has bought for us. It was not until I stopped focusing on my sins and all my failures and started focusing on my relationship with Christ that I started to really change, from the inside out. As I fell deeper in love with Jesus, I noticed my behaviors naturally changed over time. It was inevitable. Think about it – if you love someone, you want to please him or her. You trust them to know what is best for you. You begin to want to do things that bring joy to their heart, not because you *have* to but because you *want* to. You do not always get it right but you start going in the right direction.

Maybe that is why Jesus tells us in Matthew 6:33, *"Seek the Kingdom of God above all else, and live righteously, and He will give you everything you need."* If we seek Him, live for Him and trust Him for our righteousness instead of our own works, He will give us all that we need. What does it mean to "live righteously"? Well, it means to obey God. And how do we obey God? Are we capable of this? Isn't obeying God "works"?

Let's go back to the Scripture in Ezekiel 36:27, *"I will put my Spirit in you so that you will follow my decrees and be careful to obey my regulations."* This makes it very clear that He must put His Spirit in us in order for us to be able to obey Him. Without His Spirit, we are doomed! This exchange happens the moment we trust Jesus Christ as our Lord and He gives us that new heart. That spiritual heart transplant, in itself, is how God sees us as righteous. When He sees us, He sees the righteousness of Christ! Paul said in Philippians 3:9, "...*I no longer count on my own righteousness through obeying the law; rather, I become righteous through faith in Christ. For God's way of making us right with himself depends on faith.*"

Our righteousness has nothing to do with our outward behavior and everything to do with our inward condition. We have to allow God to change our selfish "want to's" to what He wants us to do! This can only happen when God changes our inward condition, when He gives us a new heart and puts His Spirit within us.

I have spoken personally with many women on this subject. Women who, like me, have struggled with addictions and behaviors that did not line up with what they said they believed about Jesus. I have heard the same things over and over again, and I remember thinking these very things...

"Why would God forgive me? My sin is so terrible!"

"Even though I'm a Christian now, I keep doing the same sins and it's actually gotten worse since I became a believer!"

"God is mad at me now – I've sinned again and now it's too late!"

"I'm not worthy."

Let's tackle these deceptions one at a time. The first one about your sin being terrible is very true. It is terrible. That is precisely why Jesus had to die, in order to pay the penalty for that horrible sin. All sin. Even the worst of it. His sacrifice was enough. You are not such a big sinner that your sin is excluded from that. God knew you would sin and He provided Jesus to pay for it. You just have to trust that, believe from your heart and receive that forgiveness, whether you feel you deserve it or not.

The second statement always makes me smile. I hear new believers say, "It's worse than it ever was! When I sin, I feel just awful and I think it has actually gotten worse!" Why would I smile about this statement? Well, it is a real indication that the Holy Spirit is inside of you. A "symptom", if you will. When He resides in you and you have a new heart, your sin *is* going to feel worse. You will begin to feel conviction over your sin and it is heart breaking. Instead of looking at it and feeling discouraged, try remembering that you are now a new creation and you will not live the way you used to anymore. This conviction is *not* an invitation to beat yourself up. It is a warning. It is an opportunity to turn away from the sin and toward the forgiveness and freedom that Christ offers. Heed the warning and receive the forgiveness He so freely gives. Deal with your sin. But remember the sin no longer *de*fines you anymore; it is now being used to *re*fine you. God says through the prophet Isaiah in Isaiah 48:10, *"I have refined you, but not as silver is refined. Rather, I have refined you in the furnace of suffering."* Sometimes that suffering is the consequences or the conviction of our sin. It can be very difficult, but Romans 8:28 reminds us that all things work together for the good for those who love God and are called according to His purpose.

The third lie about God being mad at you is one the enemy uses on many of us. If we think He's mad at us, we begin to give up because we feel like we have blown it. But remember that God took His anger out on Jesus on that cross and Jesus said,

"It is finished" before He took His last breath. It is finished. All sin is paid for. The cost was high, but it was paid for you. He loves you – He is not mad. He is "no longer counting men's sins against them" according to 2 Corinthians 5:19.

"I am not worthy," is something we all feel at some point. Truth is, we do not deserve the grace and mercy God has poured on us. But He thinks we are worth it. Who are we to say we are not? The God of the Universe thinks you are worth dying for! He is absolutely crazy about you. He knows you are not going to be righteous in your own strength, so focusing on your works instead of getting to know Him better will only lead to legalism.

Legalistic thinking can destroy our relationship with God. We will lose every time we try to measure our faith by our works. Yes, it is true that James said faith without works is dead (James 2:20). However, what we must understand is that the works are a direct result of a faith that has transformed you from the inside out. The works are a *symptom* of genuine faith, not a *precursor*. A lifestyle change without a heart change is impossible to maintain. The heart must change first. That's why it is impossible to look at someone and know from the outside what is going on in their heart. Only God can see straight into our heart. Legalism is so deceptive. You can look quite righteous on the outside and be so rotten at the core.

Our vision can get very distorted when we focus on our own works and not God's grace. Jesus had His harshest words for the "religious" and "self-righteous" folks in His day. As a matter of fact, He said some things in Matthew 23 that would make heads spin today. For instance, as He spoke to the Pharisees (religious teachers) He called them hypocrites, white-washed tombs (cleaned up on the outside but filled with death and decay on the inside), self-indulgent, greedy, blind guides, and children of hell! He also said they did things for show, they were filthy, and that the people should practice and obey what they tell them, but not to follow their example because they don't practice what they preach. *Whoa.* When you read Matthew 23, you realize why these guys wanted Jesus dead. He saw through to their wicked hearts. He saw they were frauds and He was not afraid to say it out loud. I am sure they did not like that one bit. I did not like it one bit when He revealed my wicked heart to me, either, but He gave me grace to turn from my sin and He gave me a new heart that is tender and responsive to His voice.

Why do we put these laws and burdens upon ourselves when He clearly tells us not to do this? I think I know at least one reason. I don't think we trust the Holy Spirit in us enough at times. Humor me while I share an example of this with you:

Let's say God tells us not to play in the street. So, out of our love for Him, we are obedient and decide not to play in the street. We trust Him to know what is best for us. But then someone comes along and tells us we should not play on the sidewalk, either. They might argue that if we play on the sidewalk, we might accidentally go into the street. So we play in the yard, away from the sidewalk.

A few minutes later, someone says they feel tempted to go on the sidewalk. They suggest we all go inside of the house to avoid that temptation because if we play in the sidewalk, we might accidentally go into the street. Everyone files into the house. Rather than deal with the temptation, they build another boundary around themselves.

Now we are all in the house but we are looking out the window, longingly, at the yard. So someone shuts the curtains. Why even look at the yard? I mean, if we look at the yard, we might want to go outside and then we would be tempted to play in the sidewalk that is right beside the street and God told us not to play in. We all agree we need another boundary.

Eventually, we all end up in the closet, far away from the street. We may be protected from the temptations but we are clearly not living wholehearted lives. That is what legalism does to us. It puts rules around rules. It heaps so many rules on us that we feel like we are locked in a closet. God told us not to play in the street, but because we are so afraid, we ended up in the closet. God never told us to go in the closet, though. He just said not to play in the street. If He did not think we would be strong enough to play on the sidewalk without going in the street, why wouldn't He make that clear? We created the rule because of our lack of trust in Him and in ourselves. Unfortunately, the people who are lost and do not know Jesus are in that street. The further away we get from them, the more likely they are to get run over and live eternally apart from Jesus!

Galatians 5:16-18 says, *"So I say, let the Holy Spirit guide your lives. Then you won't be doing what your sinful nature craves. The sinful nature wants to do evil, which is just the opposite of what the Spirit wants. And the Spirit gives us desires that are the opposite of what the sinful nature desires. These two forces are constantly fighting each other, so you are not free to carry out your good intentions. But when you are directed by the Spirit, you are not under obligation to the Law of Moses."*

If we truly trusted the Holy Spirit to guide our lives, if we would seek first God's Kingdom and His righteousness instead of our own, we would have everything we need – including the self-control it takes to play on the sidewalk without going into the street. Are you following me?

Someone might argue that it makes sense to follow rules to gain favor, right? But God's ways are not our ways. His ways are contrary to our human reasoning. In Isaiah 55:8-9, He says, *"My thoughts are nothing like your thoughts and my ways are far beyond anything you could imagine. For just as the heavens are higher than the earth, so my ways are higher than your ways and my thoughts higher than your thoughts."*

Focus on Him, my friend. Your rules will only lead to frustration, anger, disillusionment and bitterness. When you fall in love with Jesus and give Him your heart, you will change from the inside out. You will never be perfect on this side of heaven, but His grace and mercy are more than enough to cover your sin.

I do believe God is still working that false religion of legalism out of my heart, though. It's like "religious rehab" of sorts. Every day I realize I'm still stuck in some of my old thought patterns. It's a little different now, though. I find I'm pretty judgmental toward the *religious folks*. The ones who are still shutting people out. The ones who are turning people away because of how they look. But my being judgmental toward the "judgmental" isn't good, either. Jesus loved them enough to die for them, just like He loved and died for the most wretched "sinner".

Oh, Lord, help me.

There are quite a few of us who have been so "religionized" that we've lost sight of what really matters. Jesus came to save the broken and the lost, not the ones who think they have it all together. Even though my new heart does not want to carry out the same old habits of judging, finger wagging and being cynical, I still do them sometimes. But it grieves my heart. And I want to change. How sad to think that we may totally understand the letter of the Law, but completely miss God's heart on important issues. He is more concerned about the heart of a person than He is their behavior. We can be right about something and still be wrong because we completely miss the point when we do not handle situations with love and grace.

We all need Jesus. We are all messed up in some way. We all have sins we are dealing with. But we seem to notice the sins in others a whole lot easier than our own, don't we? Are we so worried about being "God's Gestapos" and pointing out the sins of others that we are not allowing Him to show us our own sin?

Oh, Lord, help us all.

Thankfully, He does help us. We could never do this on our own. Since there is absolutely no way we can obey the law without His Spirit, one may wonder why the Law was given in the first place. Understandable. That is why the Apostle Paul talked about this very thing with the Galatians. He said to them, *"Why, then, was the law given? It was given alongside the promise to show people their sins. But the law was designed to last only until the coming of the child who was promised."* (Galatians 3:19) Jesus is that promised child!

False teachers who were twisting the truth concerning Christ were fooling the people in Galatia. They were telling the people that salvation was more than just believing in Christ. They were telling them that in order to be saved, they had to be circumcised and they were adding a list of rules to the Galatians in order to control them. Paul did not approve of this and the entire book of Galatians is a letter Paul sent to them to help set them straight. He concludes the letter to the Galatians by saying, "It doesn't matter whether we have been circumcised or not. What counts is whether we have been transformed into a new creation." Ah, a new creation. Sounds like that new heart is what changes us, not our good works. That, my friend, is freedom in Christ!

Understand something very important here: the Ten Commandments were written on stone tablets. We read in Exodus 31:18, *"When the Lord finished speaking with Moses on Mount Sinai, He gave him the two stone tablets inscribed with the terms of the covenant, written by the finger of God."* This is our Ten Commandments; the rules God gave the people to follow in order to be made right with Him. The problem was that nobody was able to follow them because they were impossible in their sinful state to follow. Then, when Jesus came to earth, He made it even more difficult to follow the Law by saying in Matthew 5:27, *"You have heard the commandment that says, 'You must not commit adultery.' But I say, anyone who even looks at a woman with lust has already committed adultery with her in his heart."* Wow, that sure complicates things. There again, we see that it's a heart thing.

So, let's revisit Ezekiel 36:26-27, the verses I have already mentioned several times in this book so far: *"And I will give you a new heart, and I will put a new spirit in you. I will take out your stony, stubborn heart and give you a tender, responsive heart. And I will put my Spirit in you so that you will follow my decrees and be careful to obey my regulations."* Did you catch that word, "stony" in there? Our hearts are made of stone – just like those commandments that were etched out on those stones by God's finger so many years ago on Mount Sinai. When we try, in vain, to live up to God's standard on our own, we continue to be hardened to the truth – hard like that stone the Ten Commandments were etched on. Our hearts must be replaced – transplanted, if you will – by God if we are going to be transformed. *It's a heart thing.*

The next time you feel like you need to perform for God, just remember that He is not interested in your performance. He sees right through it. He is way more interested in what is going on inside – in your heart – the place where the battle begins. Let Him change your "want to's". He is able and willing to do that but we must let go of our desire to control our destinies with our behavior and trust Him with our whole heart. Letting go might seem difficult, and honestly it is until you actually do it. But once you do, the incredible grace and peace that floods you will be confirmation that you've received that tender and responsive heart – one that responds not only to laws, but to the sweet voice of Almighty God, the One who holds the stars.

Chapter Ten

Take Heart

"I have told you this so that you may have peace in me.
Here on earth you will have many trials and sorrows.
But take heart, because I have overcome the world."
John 16:33

I recall a time in my life when life seemed almost unbearable. I was a Christian and because of that, I felt almost guilty about my condition. I was going through a lot emotionally and physically and I was enveloped in darkness and depression. I mean, shouldn't Christians be perky and happy all the time? What kind of witness was I? What would people think about Jesus if they saw me suffering with depression? Was God disappointed in me?

The year 2005 was a very difficult year for me. My year began with me feeling very tired, drained and sick. After my blood work came back, the doctor realized I was severely anemic; so much, in fact, that they were very concerned. After running some more tests, they diagnosed me with uterine fibroids and said I needed a partial hysterectomy. Once I had the hysterectomy, they sent it off for a biopsy and realized I had pre-cancer of my uterus. They had caught it early, so it never did develop into full-blown cancer, but the thought of it sent shivers up my spine.

Within a couple of weeks, I was in severe pain again. More tests. They realized my gall bladder had stopped working and that it needed to come out. So, two months after my hysterectomy, I had surgery to remove my gall bladder. After this, the year was spent in and out of the hospital with a kidney infection, ovarian cysts, chronic headaches, and stomach aches. In the fall of that year, they discovered a lump in my left breast and they decided to perform surgery to remove it and biopsy it.

As I waited for the biopsy, I plummeted into a very deep darkness emotionally and spiritually. While I was going through these horrific health scares all year, I was still getting up at four in the morning to go and be a perky morning show girl on a Christian station in Charlotte, NC. I was performing; acting happy, pretending to have it all together but falling apart inside. You can only play that game for so long before you begin to break.

What is worse, I had a few listeners writing to me telling me I did not have enough faith and that was why I was suffering. I was absolutely devastated! How did they know my heart? I even had one guy write and tell me that I was a poor example because I had surgery. I should have trusted God to heal me, not the doctors, in his opinion. It was so hurtful.

As I sobbed with my face in the carpet after a very long prayer time one afternoon, I let loose cries of despair I cannot even explain. I had hit bottom and I knew it. I had my Bible right beside me opened to Psalm 40, *"I waited patiently for the Lord to help me, and He turned to me and heard my cry. He lifted me out of the pit of despair, out of the mud and the mire. He set my feet on solid ground and steadied me as I walked along. He has given me a new song to sing, a hymn of praise to our God. Many will see what He has done and be amazed. They will put their trust in the Lord."*

But where was He? Was He ever going to help me out of that pit of despair or were those words of the Psalmist not for me? What if the listeners were right and I did not have enough faith? These questions flooded my mind and I fought to remain focused on His promises. I lay there, exhausted. I felt a voice in my heart whisper, "What is the worst thing that can happen to you?" I thought about this question and began to trace the answer in my mind: Well, I could have cancer. I could have a very difficult time ahead of me. I might have to go through chemotherapy. The listeners who were so disappointed in my "lack of faith" may judge me even more. I might lose my hair. I might lose a breast. I may survive, but I might not. I might die and if I do, what then? That was when it hit me: I will go to heaven and be with Jesus forever and ever.

All of a sudden, this peace that passes understanding flooded over my entire body. I sat up, wiped my tears and began thanking God for this revelation. What on earth was I so afraid of, anyway? I recalled the words of Jeremiah in chapter 29, verse 11, *"For I know the plans I have for you"*, says the Lord, *"They are plans for good and not for disaster, to give you a future and a hope."* I chose to trust God and take Him at His word.

A couple of hours later, I received news from my doctor that the biopsy came back benign, I did not have cancer. I rejoiced but there was a part of me that knew that if God allowed cancer in my life, I would not have gone through it alone. God would have been with me every step of the way!

On the way to work the next morning, I began to think of the important lessons God taught me throughout the year and all of the things I had been through. My heart was so full of thankfulness. Once I arrived at work, within fifteen minutes, I had written a poem about my experience and within an hour, I was sharing it on the air. I received hundreds of responses from people everywhere who were blessed by the words of this poem. People who were suffering and in the middle of something difficult but were finding the peace that passes understanding. Here is the poem I wrote that fall morning in the year 2005:

They told me "Just have faith! You must believe it's true!
Because believing is the key to this illness leaving you!"

They quoted verses on healing, said Jesus
died so we wouldn't be sick;
They told me if I'd just claim it, this illness I would kick.

So I prayed and cried and wondered why
the Lord seemed so unwilling
To heal my hurting body and answer to my bidding.

My prayers I prayed unwavering and
I believed all the right verses

But instead of the hopeful blessings I
felt my life was full of curses.

Then one day as I was praying the Lord
spoke to me through a verse
He said suffering produces character and
that my life could be much worse.

He showed me that the purpose of my suffering would be
A closer walk with Him and His faithfulness I would see.

During suffering and in illness we can
draw closer to our Jesus!
And when we rely on Him for strength,
others notice and believe us.

And what speaks louder to this world
than a thankful, joyful man
Who doesn't appear to have much luck
but nonetheless can stand?

Our Lord, He draws us close when we recognize He is near
He puts His arms around us and teaches us not to fear.

The Bible makes it clear that times of suffering will come
And that He will be there holding us
through each and every one.

And another thing He tells us is that trials are in store
Because the testing of our faith will help
us grow to trust Him more!

So consider it pure joy, my friends when
we face trials of many kinds,
Our Lord has paused to teach us that
He will never leave our side.

Hold on, my friend, the healing will come
through His power and His might
It may look different than you thought,
but His ways are always right.

Our purpose in life is not to live a life of comfort and of ease
It's to become more like Jesus & our
Heavenly Father to please.

Can you relate to this poem on some level? Maybe you have been through a difficult season in life, whether it be a health scare, a divorce, the loss of a job or even a conflict within the church. No matter what we go through, it seems there are always those who, with good intentions, give us bad advice and counsel. Job had friends like that. They really thought they knew what God was doing in Job's life and why He was allowing such devastation, but at the end of the book of Job we read that God was very upset about the fact that Job's friends were so presumptious to assume they knew why God allowed such things. It's ridiculous to think we could ever know the motives of God! The only way we can get through these tough times is to trust God, no matter what. We can know that He is in control and trust Him with our lives, no matter how things may seem to look.

A believer with a new heart goes through difficulties and heartbreak just like everyone else but there are two major differences: We never go through anything alone and God can take our pain and turn it around into something with purpose. People who have not had a spiritual heart transplant do not have the presence of Christ in their life. They are not given those supernatural gifts of the Spirit of God that are deposited into every believer, according to Galatians 5:22, *"But the Holy Spirit produces this kind of fruit in our lives: love, joy, peace, patience, kindness, goodness, faithfulness, gentleness, and self control. There is no law against these things!"*

We have access to these gifts as a believer because He gave them to us, but we have to trust Him to work them out in us. The promise that God can take our pain and turn it around into something with purpose is found in Romans 8:28, *"And we know that God causes everything to work together for the good of those who love God and are called according to his purpose for them."* He said **all** things, not just some things. All things, including our pain and our heartbreak.

We will have trouble in this world, but Jesus tells us to "take heart" in John 16:33 because He has "overcome the world". *Take heart.* Did you catch that? It is an action word – we must *take* heart. Remember, the New Testament was originally written in the Greek language. The Greek word used for "take heart" was *tharseo*, which means the same as "take courage". Jesus used those same words to encourage the disciples when they were on the boat in the middle of a fierce storm. According to Matthew 14:24–27, this is the scene: *"Meanwhile, the disciples were in trouble far away from the land, for a strong wind had risen, and they were fighting heavy waves. About three o'clock in the morning, Jesus came toward them, walking on the water. When the disciples saw Him walking on the water, they were terrified. In their fear, they cried out, "It's a ghost!" But Jesus spoke to them at once, "Don't be afraid," he said. "Take courage. I am here!"*

Do you, by chance, ever feel like the disciples in this story? Life might feel like a storm, with waves crashing up and over you. You might be fighting heavy waves. The text does not mention that the disciples were afraid of the storm, though. It said they were afraid when they saw something they did not understand. They were filled with fear when they saw Jesus, but they did not recognize Him. It was not what they expected at all and it made them afraid. Sometimes in our lives, Jesus can be right there, allowing a storm in our lives, but never leaving us and never abandoning us in the midst of it. Life may not look as we expected it to look. Do we trust Him? Do we have the strength to "take courage" and trust that He is there, even when we do not understand what is going on? God never promised an easy life once we become believers and begin to follow Him. He said it would be hard, but worth it and He will never leave us or forsake us.

In Isaiah 51:1, God clearly says, *"Listen to me, all who hope for deliverance — all who seek the Lord! Consider the rock from which you were cut, the quarry from which you were mined."* What could this mean? When the temple that God was going to send His presence into was being built in the Old Testament, these were some of the instructions in building that temple (1 Kings 6:7): *"The stones used in construction of the Temple were finished at the quarry, so there was no sound of hammer, ax, or any other iron tool at the building site."* The Jewish people were very, very careful to make sure that the stones that were going to fit into the Temple they were constructing would fit perfectly. They would make the noise and chisel the stones far away from the place where the Temple was being built. Then, they would roll them slowly and careful and slip them into place. Once they were in place, they fit perfectly. The hard work of getting them to fit, though, happened at the quarry.

May I submit to you that the world represents the quarry for us? We are being "mined" in this world. This is where we are being chiseled and formed so that we will fit perfectly into the Temple being built. So, what is this "Temple" we are being built for? Ephesians 2:19-22 says, *"So now you Gentiles are no longer strangers and foreigners. You are citizens along with all of God's holy people. You are members of God's family. Together, we are his house, built on the foundation of the apostles and the prophets. And the cornerstone is Christ Jesus himself. We are carefully joined together in Him, becoming a holy temple for the Lord. Through Him you Gentiles are also being made part of this dwelling where God lives by His Spirit."*

Wow. So, we are being joined with other believers to build a Temple for the Spirit of God to dwell! But today is the hard work of being chiseled. This means our heart will break. We will experience suffering. We will experience difficulties. It will hurt. We will experience frustrations and disappointments. But we are not alone in our suffering. We have not only His Spirit, but also His people to help us through these tough times. Our pain is never in vain. Our brokenness always precedes our usefulness with God.

We are not the only ones who experience a broken heart. Think about it, if our hearts were still stone, they would be less likely to break than our new, transplanted heart of flesh. This is why, once we are believers, our sin seems so much more offensive to us. We are now tender and responsive to God's Spirit and when we sin, we grieve Him. When He grieves, we feel it. But the point I want to make is this: He grieves. His heart breaks. He hurts, too.

God is not asking us to go through anything that He has not gone through. I believe that nothing breaks God's heart more than our unbelief. Jesus wept only a few times in the New Testament. Once in John 11:35 when He saw the unbelief and grief of those who were mourning over Lazarus, once in Luke 19:41-44 when Jesus wept over Jerusalem because He knew they did not believe in Him and once in the Garden of Gethsemane the night before His crucifixion as He prayed. All three instances can be traced back to unbelief on the part of His people.

Unbelief leads to sin, pride, rebellion, a calloused heart, and legalism. When we do not believe God and take Him at His word, He cannot help us. That is why we must trust Him. It is by grace through faith that we are saved and faith means we believe in something, even when we cannot see any proof. When you fully trust and have faith in someone, you know they will not let you down. God wants us to trust Him in this way.

Have you ever felt completely broken? I sure have. It is a deep, aching sadness that is hard to explain. It feels like I've hit the bottom - or worse yet, that the bottom I hit drops out and I realize there is more depth and falling to come. Sometimes it feels dark and lonely and other times it feels desperate and out of control. No matter how it feels, though, it is real and it is a feeling we all experience at one time or another in our lives.

Maybe it is the death of a loved one that brings it on. It could also be the death of a dream, a relationship gone sour, a deep hurt from someone you love, a hurting or sick child or a burden for people you want to help but you do not know how. Maybe it is your pride that has been broken. You have felt it - we all have. But what do we do with our brokenness and how can we come out of it? Why is it that when we receive this new heart from Christ that the pain does not go away and sometimes, it even feels deeper and more intense when we hurt? Shouldn't Jesus take our pain away and give us happiness and good times?

Driving down the road one day, I heard a preacher on the radio talking about the sower and the seed from Luke 8:5-8. As he was reading the scriptures, I was praying God would help me understand them on a deeper level. I had been experiencing some brokenness in my own life due to some relationship issues and I really needed to hear from God. The preacher read these words that Jesus spoke:

"A farmer went out to sow his seed. As he was scattering the seed, some fell along the path; it was trampled on, and the birds of the air ate it up. Some fell on rock, and when it came up, the plants withered because they had no moisture. Other seed fell among the thorns, which grew up with it and choked the plants. Still other seed fell on good soil. It came up and yielded a crop, a hundred times more than was sown." When he said this, he called out, "He who has ears to hear, let him hear."

As I heard this radio preacher talk about these verses, something really struck me. We know the seed represents the Word of God - and the first person His Word came to in the story was compared to a hardened path. It was referred to as "fallow ground," which means it had been trampled on, stepped on, abused and hardened over time. It was a path that had been walked on so much that it was hard like concrete. Does this sound familiar? Is that how you might feel? Stepped on, abused or hardened by the world? Well, if this describes you, please know that things are not hopeless. And know that you are not alone!

In Jeremiah 4:3, the Lord tells the people to *"break up your unplowed ground and do not sow among thorns."* And in Hosea 10:12 the Lord says *"Sow for yourselves righteousness, reap the fruit of unfailing love, and break up your unplowed ground; for it is time to seek the Lord, until he comes and showers righteousness on you."*

Notice, it is possible for us to break up the "unplowed" or "fallowed" ground that has been trampled on, stepped on and abused by the world. Once the soil of our hearts is broken up, the seeds of righteousness can be planted deep within us! They will produce fruit. But in order to break it up, we must come to terms with being broken.

This may describe where you are right now - and you are fighting it with everything in you. No one likes to feel broken. In the world, brokenness represents a fault, something that is returned or discarded. When we purchase something and it is broken, we return it or we throw it away. But to God, brokenness is something altogether different. Check this out...

Psalm 51:17 "The sacrifices of God are a broken spirit; a broken and contrite heart, O God, you will not despise."

Psalm 34:17-18 "The righteous cry out, and the Lord hears them; he delivers them from all their troubles. The Lord is close to the brokenhearted and saves those who are crushed in spirit."

Psalm 147:3 "He heals the brokenhearted and binds up their wounds."

Isaiah 61:1-3 (prophecy concerning Jesus Christ) "The Spirit of the Sovereign Lord is on me, because the Lord has anointed me to preach good news to the poor. He has sent me to bind up the brokenhearted, to proclaim the year of the Lord's favor and the day of vengeance of our God, to comfort all who mourn, and provide for those who grieve in Zion - to bestow on them a crown of beauty instead of ashes, the oil of gladness instead of mourning, and a garment of praise instead of a spirit of despair. They will be called oaks of righteousness, a planting of the LORD for the display of His splendor."

I could go on and show you more about how God feels about our brokenness but I think you get the picture. He is drawn to those who are low in spirit, brokenhearted and humble. The crushing of our pride and our self-sufficiency is a terrifying thing unless we realize that we are trading in something weak for something much stronger - sufficiency in Him.

If you are feeling broken, allow God to plant those seeds deep within you. It can be a painful process (I know this from experience), but the hope I want to remind you of is the hope He gives you in His word by reminding you that you are not alone, you are not going through this despair for no reason and, in the words of the prophet Isaiah…*"you will be called oaks of righteousness, a planting of the LORD* **for the display of His splendor.**"

He will display His splendor in you. But brokenness always precedes usefulness with God. There is always purpose that we cannot fathom in our pain. *Trust Him.* The seeds are coming and the fruit will follow.

Chapter Eleven
Heart Motives

People may be pure in their own eyes, but
the Lord examines their motives.
-Proverbs 16:2

Are you exhausted? Are you falling into bed each night, wondering where the day went? Are you frustrated because you feel like you need to either get some help or clone yourself in order to be able to do the day-to-day tasks in your life? When is the last time you spent quality time with your family? This doesn't include watching the kids play sports or taking the family on a business trip - I'm talking face-to-face family time with no distractions.

I get it. I really, really get it. I'm the Queen of Over-Commitment Syndrome. My mentor once told me, "Leslie, if you are exhausted or overwhelmed, you are probably doing something God has not asked you to do." I believe she is absolutely right. And God is teaching me some tough truths as He allows me, by His grace, to see the motivations behind some of my commitments.

Let's explore this a bit:

- You've just been asked to take over a ministry or a committee and even though you know it's more than you can handle, you justify saying yes because you are sure that nobody else will do it, and if they do, they probably won't do it the way you would and that would make things harder for you.
- You've just been asked to take on more responsibility at work and even though it cuts into your family time even more, you go ahead and commit to it without even blinking because it might get you ahead in the company.
- You want your child to be well rounded, so you have them in dance class, sports, drama team and they are active in the youth group. You barely ever see them and usually dinner is on the run, but they will be very prepared for life in the future, so you justify the busyness as a small price to pay for future success in your child's life.

These are examples of decisions we all face every single day. The question is: How do we know we've made the right decision? How can we be sure that when we commit to doing something that we are motivated by our heart and not our desire to keep up with others, to prove ourselves, to make more money or to make a name for ourselves or our children?

After hitting the wall about a million times in my life, I'm learning to simplify my life by taking a look at what matters most. I listed out my top three priorities. Once I did this, I began to ask myself some important questions:

1. What does God think about this? (I pray first...so important)

2. What does my husband think about this? He is the voice God uses very often in my life to help me balance my life - he sees things clearly when I can get emotionally blinded or selfish.

3. Will this activity cut into my priorities?

4. Will this activity enhance time spent with my priorities?

5. Can I honestly say I'm doing this because it's the right thing to do or is there another motive in there somewhere?

6. If I do this, what are the possible domino effects down the line in the future?

7. Are there any other options or creative compromises I can do to make this more feasible in my life?

I'm finally realizing that if my top three priorities get pushed aside in order to fulfill commitments made outside of them, I suffer and so does my family and my relationship with God. I envision my priorities being protected by a big, inpenetrable wall of protection. First, my relationship with God. Second, my relationship with my husband and finally, my children.

When these things are protected, I can make a much wiser decision. It's been a difficult transition and I can honestly say I'm really not there yet. But when I consider the consequences of over-commitment and resulting neglect in my top three priorities, I begin to understand the importance of protecting them. When my relationship with God is neglected, everything else falls apart. My relationship with Him is what fuels me - the love I have for others and the good motivations of my heart to serve others can only come from His love flowing through me. In my own strength, I become exhausted.

I also find that when I struggle with a selfish motive, I end up not being faithful. I feel like the hare in the story of *The Tortoise and the Hare*. Just to remind you, the hare may have been quick and impressive out of the starting gate, but he didn't finish the race. I feel like I can get very zealous for things and begin running toward the finish line, only to get exhausted and distracted, stopping along the path in order to rest. Meanwhile, my passion fizzles, I become bitter and exhausted and my heart begins to change. That was why I prayed and asked God, "Why do I do this?"

The beginning of this answer began when I was reading Matthew 23:23:

"Woe to you, teachers of the law and Pharisees, you hypocrites! You give a tenth of your spices—mint, dill and cumin. But you have neglected the more important matters of the law—justice, mercy and faithfulness. You should have practiced the latter, without neglecting the former."

Did you catch that? Jesus spoke these words and He said the more important matters were justice, mercy and faithfulness.

Faithfulness. That was what I lacked. How had I missed this?

I've read this verse many times but never caught that word mixed in there like that. I was so convicted. This verse would not let me go - all day it ran through my mind. I had a checklist going in my head about all the things I'd started and not finished.

At first, I was overwhelmed with what other people must think of me, but I quickly remembered that it was not my concern what anyone else might think. I knew God wasn't pleased and that's all that mattered. The more I worried about what others thought, the more I lost focus of what He was trying to accomplish in my life through this difficult realization.

I'm thrilled to say that even though this was a hard lesson to learn, it was a good one. God has shown me why I don't finish sometimes. He has also reminded me, very mercifully I might add, of all the things I have finished and continue to press toward, faithfully. I love how He balances things out so I'm not overwhelmed with all I'm doing wrong by throwing in the things I'm actually doing right.

If you have committed to something and you are at the point where you feel like giving up, I suggest you ask yourself a few questions before doing so:

1. **What was my motive for beginning the task in the first place?** If your answer is "because nobody else would do it", "because I couldn't say no to him/her", "because I want to be needed" or "because nobody else can do it as well as I can", you are in for some trouble.

The motive for doing something, for serving, for giving of your time must always come from a heart of obedience to what God is calling you to do. If we want to be faithful, we must be sure that we are walking in His will and doing what He wants us to do, otherwise we are working in our own strength and we will lose heart. Ask Him to examine your motive before making commitments. Proverbs 16:2 *"People may be pure in their own eyes, but the Lord examines their motives."*

2. **Did I pray about it and seek wise counsel before deciding to do the task?** Sometimes my biggest problem comes from committing to do something that I've not prayed about or talked with my husband and/or mentor about. I hear of a need and I jump to fill it because it seems like the right thing to do and I enjoy serving. I go in with full fervor and then fizzle out within weeks. Even if things "seem" to be right, we must pray. You must be in agreement with your spouse and/or seek wise counsel before committing to do something. Proverbs 12:15 *"Fools think their own way is right, but the wise listen to others."*

3. **Am I doing this because I think God needs me to?** I believe we often subconsciously think, "What would God do without me?" When in reality, God is perfectly capable of filling a position! He is God – He is powerful and He is not desperate for our help. He gives us opportunities to help, but just like when our kids "help us" in the kitchen, it would probably be easier if He just did it by Himself! But He loves us and He gives opportunities to help for us to grow, learn and

become more like Jesus. But, just like if our kids tried to do it all, they would quickly become discouraged and overwhelmed, when we try to do it all, we do the same.

4. **Did I hurry through the decision making process?** Whew, this is a big one...did you give yourself time in making a decision to commit? If not, you may have acted hastily. Personally, I've decided to implement a three-day period of prayer and counsel prior to making a decision to serve in a specific area. This gives me time to consider, to calm down from all of my initial excitement and zeal to "save the world" and helps me to slow down. I have seen, time and time again, that hasty decisions are usually not the right ones. Slow down, give yourself time, and if the person asking you doesn't grant you the time to pray about it and seek wise counsel, then you probably don't want to work with them anyway. Proverbs 19:2 *"Enthusiasm without knowledge is no good; haste makes mistakes."*

5. **Am I being led by the Spirit of God?** This is huge. If I am being led by the Spirit, I will not gratify the desires of my flesh (Galatians 5:16). If He is leading me and the task is something He wants me to do, I will have the power within me to finish. I will be given supernatural strength, fervor and determination. Otherwise, I'm working in my own strength. We all know that without Him leading us, we will not succeed. He must be the One we follow. Not the opinions of others, not the approval of others and not the manipulations of others (including our own selves). If you are led by Him, your

motivation will be a pure heart-motive that overflows from a love and compassion for what you are doing – not a desire to fill a role or be someone important.

6. **Am I giving up too easily?** Sometimes we are absolutely called to do something, but then things get hard. We begin to feel like we cannot possibly make a difference – we are just one person. But God says our hard work will be rewarded. He says there is much to be gained by our faithfulness in not only the big things, but also the small things. If you are doing what God has called you to do, you can still find yourself becoming discouraged when things seem difficult or impossible. Galatians 6:9 reminds us: *"Let us not become weary in doing good, for at the proper time we will reap a harvest if we do not give up."* Ask God for His help to persevere. Your faith may be tested, but James 1:3 says that will give your endurance an opportunity to grow. Never, never, never, never give up. He is faithful, even when we are not (2 Timothy 2:13).

A verse that is often misunderstood and misquoted comes from Psalm 37:4, *"Take delight in the Lord, and He will give you your heart's desires."* Some people think that means if we delight ourselves in the Lord, He'll give us everything we want. In a round about way that could be construed as true, but actually what this verse is really saying is that if God is the deepest delight of our heart, He will implant His desires into ours. He changes our heart's desires. A spiritual heart transplant.

As you can see, we can do a lot of really good things for a lot of really bad reasons. When we are careful in the beginning to make the right decision and our motive is something that flows from a changed heart, we will be equipped and ready to fulfill whatever the job may be. God will never ask you to do something for which He has not equipped you. And His desire is that we do not just do good things, but that we do "God" things – things that He planned, in advance, for us to do.

Our motives may seem right to us, but God sees our heart. One of the bravest and scariest prayers we can pray is for God to reveal our true heart-motives to us. I do not want to play games anymore and honestly, sometimes I am so good at games that I can even fool myself.

We've spent a great deal of time in this chapter talking about our hidden motives in decision making and commitments, but we must also spend some time talking about motives in our treatment of others. I was shown a very ugly side of myself one day when we went to church a few years ago.

We had one of those crazy mornings getting ready for church and honestly, we were not in very good moods by the time we arrived. We couldn't find socks, we were running late, we fought over who was going to feed the dog and let him out and we were sour faced and cranky. Of course, we put the "church face" on as we filed out of the mini-van on that sunny Sunday morning. But my son, Tommy, was not going to put the face on. He was much too authentic for that. So, he moped around the church, looked down and slouched as he endured the hour-long service. He didn't say a word, but his body-language was shouting out, "I don't want to be here!" as loud as it could.

As I glanced over at him, I began to look around to see if anyone was looking at him, judging our family and my son.

It was then I noticed a woman I had never seen there before staring at him, looking like she felt sorry for him. Oh, I was livid!

After the service, she approached us and asked me if my son was okay. I smiled and thanked her for her concern and said he would be fine. But I was fuming inside as we walked back to the mini-van. My mind was going a hundred miles an hour, thinking about how my son had embarrassed me. I mean, I was a *Christian* speaker, writer and radio host! Would anyone want to hear or read a word I had to say if they knew I couldn't even get my own son to listen to me? Why was he doing this to me!? Oh, I was getting angrier by the moment.

Once the doors were safely shut and we began to pull out of the parking lot, my plastic, smiley face was gone and replaced by an annoyed, ugly person who began to unleash my anger and embarrassment on my son with a passionate fit of anger! I really let him have a piece of my mind! As I finished up my furious discourse, my final words were, *"Couldn't you just pretend to be happy?!"*

Tommy didn't speak. I think he knew better! He just stared straight ahead and immediately I felt tremendous conviction. Why was I so mad at him anyway? It hit me. *I just told my son to pretend.* I was teaching my son to play the church game – the very game that I hated so much. I looked out the window and silently, the tears fell from my eyes. I was so ashamed. My motive was not to help him. My motive was selfish. I was more concerned about my reputation and how people would perceive me than I was for my son and what he was going through.

When we arrived at home, I asked him if I could take him to

lunch. It was there I apologized to him and asked him to forgive me. We had a wonderful talk over lunch and I realized he was dealing with a lot of stuff in his life and that was why he was hurting. He was not trying to embarrass me — I think he was just trying to get me to notice that he was hurting. But I was so wrapped up in "me" that I almost missed it. My motive was revealed to me, and as painful as that was, I'm so thankful. God, in his mercy, not only taught me an important lesson that day, but He also gave me the opportunity to make it up to my son and hear him share his heart with me.

If we knew the motive behind all of our actions and decisions, we'd probably be mortified at times. But God is so sweet to teach us by revealing these things to us and giving us opportunities to make it right.

Lord, give us eyes to see where our motives are truly coming from! And please pour out your grace and mercy on us as we are confronted with those dark areas of our heart. We want to live wholeheartedly for You.

Psalm 26:2: *Put me on trial, LORD, and cross-examine me. Test my motives and my heart.*

Chapter Twelve

A Humble Heart

When the Lord saw their change of heart, he gave this message to Shemaiah: "Since the people have humbled themselves, I will not completely destroy them and will soon give them some relief." 2 Chronicles 12:7

Quite a few years back, before I was on the radio, I took a job as a server at a local restaurant. My husband had just lost his job and we were in a situation where we needed some extra income. I was such a brat about it at first! The first two weeks I felt sorry for myself, cried on the way to and from work and thought how unfair it was that I "had to do this". When people we knew would come into the restaurant I would beg other servers to take the table if it was assigned to me because I was humiliated. I'm embarrassed as I recall my ungodly attitude about it.

I was in my quiet time one morning and God spoke to me

through Colossians 3:23, *"Work willingly at whatever you do, as though you were working for the Lord rather than for people."* As soon as I read that verse, I knew I needed to change my attitude. I needed to be grateful God provided me with a job. Many people did not have one. I found one quickly and it was close to home and it was bringing in good money for us. I needed to work as if it was the most important job on the earth and I needed to show God that I could be faithful with the small things. I felt He was telling my heart that if I would humble myself and work hard, He would honor that.

Within a month, I was promoted to the lead server, my attitude changed and I began to see a change in the people around me. It still amazes me how a change in attitude can make a job go from a chore to joy in such a short time. We began to pull together and work as a team and morale went up in the entire restaurant. It was bittersweet when just nine months later I left my waitress job to become the co-host for the Morning Show on the local Christian radio station. God honored my obedience and now I was in a job I had always dreamed of having! Funny though, as much as I love radio, I still miss waiting tables sometimes. It was fun, challenging and I lost a lot of weight with all that running around!

It's been awhile since all of that happened, but God reminded me recently that He expects me to serve joyfully - *no matter what the job is* - even if it is a job that is tedious, unglamorous, or difficult (yes, I was cleaning my bathroom when the thought came to me). When I do it with joy, people notice and my attitude changes from "having to" to "getting to". We are blessed to be able to work with our hands. *Every job counts.*

Proverbs 18:12 reminds us that pride goes before destruction but humility precedes honor. We have all seen this in action, haven't we? It is usually a matter of time before the prideful, haughty people get what the world calls "karma". We know better, though. It is not karma; it is a biblical principle. The Bible makes it clear that God is all knowing. He sees through us – right to the heart of who we are. James 4:6 says, *"As the Scriptures say, 'God opposes the proud but favors the humble'."* The God of the Universe actually opposes the prideful heart. But He shows favor to those with a humble heart. I don't know about you, but I would like the favor of God rather than the opposition of Him. So how do we become humble in heart?

Remember back in the show *Happy Days* when the Fonz was trying to admit he was wrong about something and he just couldn't get the words out? I always thought that was so funny. Until I realized I was doing the same thing in my life. Admitting we are wrong takes guts - and humility. And admitting we are wrong is the first step to true repentance. A repentant heart is a humble heart.

When I say that word "repent", does it make you think of the wild-looking guy on the street corner with a wide eyes yelling at everyone to "Repent!" while he carries a sign on him that says "The end is near!" Yeah, I used to think that, too. I didn't really understand what the word really meant, but I knew it seemed "overused" and "exaggerated" in the fire and brimstone preaching that Hollywood exploited in movies and entertainment. But not anymore.

That was what was missing in my "Counterfeit Christianity" - true repentance. I believed Jesus was who He said He was and I knew He died on the cross. I even acknowledged I was a sinner. I never really understood that repentance was such a big deal, though. It took twenty years of my life to realize that I was missing this important and crucial element, and once I finally repented from my sin, I was finally able to embrace a true relationship with Christ as Lord and Savior of my life. Believing in Jesus was simply not enough – I had to believe in Him enough that my life was surrendered to Him and His leading.

I am shocked at how often the Gospel is presented without a true presentation of what repentance is, because without it, there is no salvation. I read a book by John MacArthur called *The Gospel According to Jesus*. There is a chapter on repentance and what it means, and what it doesn't mean. I literally put the book down after marking up just about the entire chapter and yelled out "Amen!!" He makes it very clear that repentance is essential and describes what it really means – and what it does not mean. The book really helped me a lot and I highly recommend it for anyone who may be confused about it.

I can clearly see why we hate the word *repent* so much. It completely goes against our human will to be "right" and it requires great humility, something rare and difficult in these days of "I'm right, you're wrong" and "It's not my fault!" It requires surrender of our lives to Christ's Lordship - something that also takes great humility and trust. In today's world, it almost seems ridiculous that anyone would ever do any of this:

- Admit wrongdoing by assuming personal responsibility for our sin

- Take entire blame without passing it on to someone else
- Surrender to someone else's way of life besides our own
- Give up trying to control our own destiny
- Trust anyone wholeheartedly
- Obey anyone else – I mean, we are the boss, right? Who knows better than us how to live?

I remember thinking "If God didn't want me to sin, why would He make me this way?" and so I would continue to live a life of self-centeredness, living for my own purposes and pleasures. I was not taking personal responsibility. I was blaming God for my sin by accusing Him of making me a sinner. But when I realized He did not make me a sinner, but that I was born into a sinful world that was corrupt, I realized that He made me to be anything but a sinner – and that He had provided a way for me to live the life He intended for me – through Jesus Christ. But I had to get over my pride and my lack of personal responsibility and repent of my waywardness. I had to stop saying "I'm sorry" and say, "I'm through". God opposed me and my world came crashing down. I am so thankful for His opposition. It is what helped me to see my deepest need was Him.

So, you see, that is why we hate the word repent. We can't get around the fact that Jesus said, "repent" many times in the Bible – and He meant it. I think it is the true test. The place where Jesus looks us in the eyes and says, "Are you in?" and we are then faced with a decision that may seem impossible on the surface, but once we turn our backs and walk toward Christ and away from our sin, He empowers us to live righteously – not perfectly – but righteously because He can then be our righteousness for us – something we are incapable of being without Him.

Repentance is not a work we perform. Works do not get us to heaven, not at all. Repentance is just a turning away from sin and toward the Savior, letting Him do the work for us because we are completely incapable of doing it ourselves. We get no credit for this at all. All the credit goes to Him. In 2 Corinthians 7:9, Paul reminds us that even repentance is something that God initiates in us – read this carefully..."*Now I am happy, not because you were made sorry, but because your sorrow led you to repentance. For you became sorrowful as God intended and so were not harmed in any way by us. Godly sorrow brings repentance that leads to salvation and leaves no regret, but worldly sorrow brings death.*"

Those verses reiterate that God is the one who initiates repentance in a person. Godly sorrow is genuine sorrow that leads to repentance. It makes us realize we are wrong, we have offended the Holy God and we are in need of a Savior. Worldly repentance makes us sad and sorry, but not for the sin – for being caught! Godly sorrow takes humility. We realize, very quickly, that repentance seems a lot harder to do before we actually take the step – and that once we do, it is truly the best decision we could have ever made for our lives and He makes it worth every single moment.

Oh, but getting to this place can be so hard!

When I was a little girl, if I would fall down and cut myself, my mother would instantly break out the Macuracomb. Do you remember this stuff? I would cringe at the mention of it and tried to hide my cuts most of the time because I wanted to avoid it. Macuracomb was an antiseptic that was used on cuts and abrasions that stung like crazy when it touched an open wound! My mother would blow on it and try to ease my pain, but there was no way around it. I had to trust her. To be honest, the ones I tried to ignore most often became infected and caused more pain than if I had just let her use the Macuracomb on it in the first place! As much as I hated it at the time, I am so thankful my mom used that horrible stuff on me because I know without it I could have gotten much worse. It was pain with a very important purpose.

When you hear or read God's word and it stings a bit, look at that as the first indication that something may need some cleaning out in your life. I have found that the harder things sting my heart when I am reading God's word, the more likely it would be to become "infected" if He did not treat it with His truth. Can you relate to this? Have you ever read God's word and just wanted it to say something else? Maybe you wish you could just cut out a certain passage because it was just too hard to face the truth. No matter your situation, I want to encourage you that it is pain with a purpose. We can be sure of this – God knows your pain and will reveal areas where you need His healing touch of truth only when He knows the pain has a very important purpose.

It takes a great deal of humility to admit when we are wrong. Our human, flesh-tendency is to get defensive and to "protect" ourselves. In reality, this road does way more damage than good. There is an example in the Bible with King Hezekiah. In Isaiah 37, we read about his reaction to some slander that he found out some men were saying about him and about his God. In verse 14, it says, *"After Hezekiah received the letter from the messengers and read it, he went up to the Lord's Temple and spread it out before the Lord. And Hezekiah prayed this prayer before the*

Lord: O Lord of Heaven's Armies, God of Israel, you are enthroned between the mighty cherubim! You alone are God of all the kingdoms of the earth. You alone created the heavens and the earth. Bend down, O Lord, and listen!"

Two things stand out about this passage. First, I noticed he totally humbled himself by starting his prayer with statements of how great God is. He immediately stated that he knew God was greater than anything. Second, I noticed he did not take the slander and call his best friend. He did not update his Facebook status about his situation or ask for anyone else's opinion. No, King Hezekiah "spread it out before the Lord". Basically, he took his issue before God and wanted to know if any of it was true. Once he realized it was slander, he was ready to act and to act in humility and with respect for God's ways rather than the vengeance and bitterness that can often come when we ask others for their opinions. His heart was ready and willing to hear from God alone. Oh, how I want this to be true for me!

Our heart will be humble toward God or God will humble it. No matter what, God knows we must have a humble heart. For God opposes the proud, but gives grace to the humble.

Chapter Thirteen

Heart Attack

Stay alert! Watch out for your great enemy, the devil. He prowls around like a roaring lion, looking for someone to devour. 1 Peter 5:8

"You must be doing something right, when you get the devil all uptight." She said it to me with a hearty laugh at the end of her obvious joke. I suspected there was some truth in what she said though, because it made complete sense. A strong believer and very good friend, she had come over to console me after we had received some hard news and I felt hopeless. I really hope you have a friend like that in your life – one who will point you to the truth, be there to comfort you and offer you a shoulder to cry on every now and then.

It had only been about two months since Rod and I surrendered our lives to the Lord and things were not going as "planned". My husband had just come home from work and had a very distraught look on his face. I had never seen this look before and I knew it was serious. He had lost his job and sadly, I believe he also lost a part of his sense of self in the process. My husband had worked so hard to get to his current position in upper management at work and for years, I think that was how he identified himself. Yes, he was a father and a husband, but his pride and identity were in his work for many years. I can look back now and clearly see that God was teaching him as well as all of us a very important lesson: we could not put our hopes, our dreams, or our identity in anything but Him alone. But how would we cope? How would we ever get past this difficulty? We had four children to support!

Our immediate response was panic. We began to wonder about the faithfulness of God for the first time. The temptations to doubt God were overwhelming. But after spending time in prayer and consulting some spiritually strong friends for counsel, we began to feel peace that passes understanding in our situation. We began to trust God in ways we had never even known possible as we trusted that He had a plan for our lives, not to harm us but to give us hope and a future (Jeremiah 29:11).

We began to accept and even embrace our new reality when one night Rod approached me and put my hand on his neck. There was a huge lump on the right side. We looked at each other and knew right away that it was not normal. Why is it that when you feel a lump somewhere, you immediately go to the other side of your body and feel for a lump in the same place? If there is one on both sides, you breathe a sigh of relief. If not, you know it could be very bad. There was no lump on the left side. I swallowed hard and said, "We're in this together.

We're going to be okay." He smiled and we held each other, both knowing a new battle was about to begin.

The doctor was very concerned. I am pretty sure he thought it was cancer based on how quickly he reacted at the appointment. He wanted to do surgery right away to biopsy the lump, so we scheduled it that week. After what seemed like an eternity, the doctor came out and told me with a look of relief that it was not cancer; however, it was not all good news. Rod had an autoimmune disease called Sarcoidosis. He tried to explain what that meant to me but I do not think I heard a word he said because my heart was beating so fast and I was so glad it wasn't cancer.

When we went home and looked up what Sarcoidosis was, we realized this was something Rod would have to fight for the rest of his life. His diet and exercise would need to change and he would probably have flare-ups that would make him tired and weak. If he ever came down with a lung infection, it could be very bad news, so we would have to keep him healthy. We were scared, but again, we began to feel that peace that passes understanding. It was miraculous to say the least.

Nothing seemed to be going right since the night of our surrender to Jesus Christ, but oddly, we had never been more filled with joy. Knowing God was in control and feeling the love and support of our new church family took our faith to new levels. When Rod and I look back at this time in our lives, we both have fond memories. That's how God works, you know. He takes the things that are difficult in our lives and he uses those times to really teach us about His faithfulness. He brings such good out of our hard times that afterward, we can look back and see how He was there, providing for us and molding us all along.

It was a long year and a half of our lives while my husband looked for a job, but it was also one of the most beautiful times in our lives. Rod spent time with the children really getting to know them on a deeper level. He was taking them to school and picking them up, he was there for them to tuck them in and read to them at night. He was present in their lives for the very first time and he loved every moment. I was working hard to help make ends meet. We spent more time together as a couple and we began to dream together for the very first time in years. It was like we were newlyweds! I was getting to know my husband in new ways and I absolutely loved seeing him spending time with the kids.

When this all started, I would be the one going to work and he would be very adamant that the kids could be trained to pick up around the house better than when I was at home with them. For two weeks, I would come home to a clean home, dinner, bathed and perfect-looking kids. His mantra was, "No fun until the work is done!" The kids were like little trained soldiers. It was humiliating for me. I felt like a big fat loser of a mom while he made it look so easy and everything was done so easily and precisely. I began to wonder if maybe I should work and he should stay at home.

Fast forward to the third week. Suddenly, all of that changed. I came home to a complete and total disaster! The house was a mess, the kids were unruly and there were no groceries, no clean clothes and Rod looked like he hadn't slept in years. He looked at me with exhaustion in his eyes and announced, "This is hard! How do you do it?" As soon as you clean it up, they mess it up again. I can't do this anymore!" As sad as I was for him, I must say that I found a bit of twisted pleasure in knowing he was finally realizing how hard it was to be a stay-at-home parent. We knew immediately that it was time for him to get serious about finding a job. I wanted to be home with the kids more and he, well, let's just say he was ready to find a job.

One day, I passed by his study where he was working and saw a huge poster on the wall where he had drawn out his plans for the future. Step by step, he knew exactly where he wanted to go and who he wanted to be with each passing year. As I looked it over, tears filled my eyes and I asked him, "Honey, what if this is not God's plan for you? What if it's Rod's plan?" He became very quiet and after a few moments, he ripped the huge poster off the wall and said, "You're right. I'm trying too hard to run my life! God can do that just fine without me." We prayed together and asked God to take the reigns. We asked him to give us courage to trust Him with our lives. We asked for forgiveness. We held each other and sobbed. It was an incredibly unforgettable moment – one I will always treasure.

Within a couple of weeks, Rod found a job. But he never went back to his "plan". Funny thing is, as we look back over the past ten years, we can see that much of what he put on that "plan" on the wall has come to pass – but in God's timing, not Rod's timing.

Life seemed to be a lot harder since we received our new hearts. Before that spiritual heart transplant, we had never seen such hardships. That is why my friend's advice was funny, but true — *You must be doing something right when you get the devil all uptight!*

Honestly, if you really think about it, the devil has no interest in you until you have that new spiritual heart. Until that moment, you are not a threat to him. Now that you are a new creation, the enemy knows you have incredible potential to be used by God to share with others about this incredible truth of a new life. Especially when they see you living it out. Of course he's upset! But he can only attack your new heart in ways that God can use to bring glory to Himself and bring good into your life. God is the Redeemer — meaning that He can take all things and work them together for good (Romans 8:28) in your life. When you keep an eternal perspective instead of a temporal perspective, you can clearly see how God can weave His purposes through not only your victories but also your pain in life.

Another form of heart attack the enemy will bring to your new spiritual heart is temptation to sin. So, knowing your new spiritual heart is now prone to attacks of doubt, frustration and sin, you may be wondering what you can do to help fight these attacks. This chapter was written not only to let you know it's normal and we all go through these times, but it was also written to help equip you to fight. In fighting, however, it is important to remember that we do not fight the way we used to before our spiritual heart transplant. Paul reminds us in 2 Corinthians 10:3-5, *"We are human, but we don't wage war as humans do. We use God's mighty weapons, not worldly weapons, to knock down the strongholds of human reasoning and to destroy false arguments. We destroy every proud obstacle that keeps people from knowing God. We capture their rebellious thoughts and teach them to obey Christ."*

God's powerful weapon is His Word. The Bible is our only offensive weapon in fighting off the enemy. It is what Jesus used in Matthew 4 when the devil tempted Jesus to sin. He quoted scripture and the enemy could not argue. Eventually, he went away and angels came to attend to Jesus. Knowing God's Word is one of the greatest things you can do to help prevent a heart attack.

My friend, Jeannie, has to take medication every single day to help fight off rejection in her new physical heart. Your prescription is to be taken daily, as well. But it's not a pill, it is time spent alone with God in His Word, learning His ways so that you can "destroy every proud obstacle that keeps people from knowing God" and so you can "capture rebellious thoughts and teach them to obey God". Nothing can stand against God's Word.

If you take a look at Ephesians 6, Paul teaches us about the Armor of God. The Armor of God is serious stuff. Satan is a powerful enemy and we need God's power to be able to stand against him. Ephesians 6:10-17 reminds us to *put on* the Armor of God. This is an action on our part. We have a part in this – it will not just jump onto us, we must be intentional and put it on ourselves.

If you think about it, Christ represents every piece of the armor. Christ is the Way, the Truth & the Life (The Belt of Truth), Christ is our righteousness (Breastplate of Righteousness), Christ is our peace (Shoes of Peace), Christ's faithfulness makes our faith possible (Shield of Faith), Christ's sacrifice makes our salvation possible (Helmet of Salvation) and Christ is known as the Word of God in human form, so He also represents our one and only offensive weapon- the Scriptures (Sword of the Spirit). He is our Armor, my friend. We must "put Him on" each day.

Christ is our Protector, our Defender and our Righteousness. When, in humility, we remember this, we are able to fight the enemy. Actually, He is able to fight the enemy *through* us. When we know His Word, we begin to know His thoughts and His ways so we are able to fight the evil, sinful thoughts that want to overtake us. I once heard a pastor say: *the scene of the crime is in the mind.* I believe this is true. And it is also Biblical.

James talks about it in the book of James, chapter 1, verses 14-15. *"Temptation comes from our own desires, which entice us and drag us away. These desires give birth to sinful actions. And when sin is allowed to grow, it gives birth to death."* So where do our temptations begin? In our mind. Where do our desires come from? Our mind. When sin is allowed to grow, it gives birth to death. *Allowed.* Did you get that? Sin needs our *permission!* We have a choice! If we do not allow it to grow, it will not grow. If we feed the desire and continue to think in the direction of the temptation, we will sin.

There is hope here, though. Remember how we discussed that new, tender and responsive heart that God gave you when you surrendered your heart to Him? That means you will be responsive to His gentle voice of conviction. You will know when you are going the wrong way and you will be faced with a choice. Will you choose death or life?

Philippians 4:8 is a wonderful Scripture that you can think

about when you have a thought come into your mind. Paul says: *Fix your thoughts on what is true, and honorable, and right, and pure, and lovely, and admirable. Think about things that are excellent and praiseworthy...then the God of peace will be with you.* So the next time you have a thought and you are not sure it is a good one from God, give it the Philippians 4:8 test: Is the thought true? Honorable? Right? Pure? Lovely? Admirable? Excellent? Praiseworthy? If it is none of those things, it is not from God and you can, according to 2 Corinthians 10:5, *capture the rebellious thought and teach it to obey Christ!*

Remember, according to 1 Peter 5:8, the enemy is *like a roaring lion, seeking whom he may devour.* Notice, it does not say he **is** a roaring lion. It clearly says he is **like** a roaring lion. He has no power against a believer, but he wants us to believe he does. He is an intimidator with no control over us when we stand on the truth of God's Word. He cannot take our salvation away from us, so he is going to do all he can to render us powerless and destroy our testimony. Keep in mind; he comes as an angel of light in most cases, not a scary pitch-fork carrying ghoul in a red suit!

Sin always seems enticing and thrilling at the moment. It looks good, feels good, seems good, and it may even be fun for the moment, but according to James 1, it will eventually give birth to death. Death of a relationship. Death of a testimony. Death of confidence. Death of security. Death of trust. It will eventually bring about death in your life because once the pleasure runs out, the person has to seek out more and more in order to be "fulfilled". Sin is finite, so the pleasure always runs out.

However, making the right choice and deciding not to commit

the sin will be the hardest thing to do. It seems impossible. It doesn't seem fun or enticing for the moment. It doesn't seem fun for the moment, but it will give birth to life in your heart. God's pleasures and blessings are infinite – they never run out. The joy is ongoing and it lasts forever! So, I suppose you could say sin gives pleasure for a moment, but ultimately delivers death; but righteous living gives pleasure for eternity but is hard in the moment.

You have a choice now. You are not a slave to sin anymore, you are righteous and you have the ability to choose the right thing. Before your new heart, you did not have this choice. A tender and responsive heart will know what is right. The question is, will we "put on Jesus" and trust Him in those times of temptation?

We do not always make the right choice, though. About four years after Jesus gave my new heart to me, I found myself in a very public situation where I made the wrong choice. What are we supposed to do when we make the wrong choice?

It was day eight on the reality show I was competing in and we were in yet another physical reward challenge. I was already frustrated because for some reason, the show I finally get selected for turns out to be one of the most physical one-on-one combative seasons to date. Most of the challenges I'd seen on the show were a team effort in the past. Not this season. We were doing hand-to-hand combat, one on one and it was the hardest thing I had ever done.

This challenge on day eight was one of the hardest yet. We were on a makeshift boat and had to literally wrestle each other and try to fling the other tribe, one by one, off the boat into the nasty lake water. It was women against women, men against men. I had been very sick since day two and at this point, I was so weak I knew that I would have to dig deep for strength.

The show's host signaled for the challenge to begin and I almost burst into tears as I saw the three young girls from the opposing tribe coming at me. We wrestled and fought and as we did, I could feel that some of the girls were pulling on our clothing, trying to distract us so we would try to cover ourselves up instead of fighting. I couldn't help but tug at my clothes with one hand, trying to keep myself covered while wrestling with the other hand. My other two tribe mates had already been flung into the water and I was the last one standing for the first round. Before long, three girls from the other tribe came after me and flung me as hard as they could into the lake. They won round one.

We had a couple more rounds in this challenge and I was physically and emotionally spent. One of the members of my tribe was yelling at me to stop fussing with my clothing. She said it was a distraction from the fight and that I shouldn't worry if they stripped my clothes off. It was a competition – who cares who sees you at this point? She was definitely angry with me. But I couldn't help it. I was not there to strip naked on national television. It's easy to forget that 15 million people are going to be watching you at some point when you are out there fighting for your life in the jungle. But I knew it was not something I wanted to do.

As a believer in Jesus Christ, I put high expectations on myself to represent Him well. And when I would mess up, I was so hard on myself. That's probably why, after the third round of this combative challenge, as I was being flung into the nasty lake water for the last time, losing the challenge (and almost my clothes), I yelled out an expletive word that I regretted the moment it left my mouth! I hit the water and swam to the side of the boat where I just wept uncontrollably. There I was, wrestling with other women and screaming out a word that I should not be screaming, much less on national television. This was not what I signed up for.

One of my tribe mates and dear friends out there, Courtney, helped me out of the water and asked me what was wrong. When I explained to her that I had just said a word I wished I hadn't said on national television, she laughed, hugged me and told me to shake it off. But I couldn't. I felt just horrible. *I was a mother, a Christian speaker and radio host.* I really felt I had blown my witness. They would show this on national television and everyone watching would judge me and possibly even judge my God based on my behavior! What if they fired me at the radio station? I put the weight of the world on my shoulders.

I was so distracted by beating myself up that I didn't even realize my tribe was plotting to vote me out that night. When we focus on our sin and not our Savior, a lot of things can go unnoticed in our lives, you know. Once I was voted out, I lost many hours of sleep, re-playing that moment in my head over and over and wishing I hadn't said what I said. I was tired. Sick. Exhausted. Upset. Would any of that matter to the millions of people watching? Would they ever understand?

I asked the Lord for forgiveness and honestly, I felt He forgave me before I even finished asking. But I couldn't forgive myself.

I continued to re-live the moment for months – until the show aired in October of 2007.

While watching the scene, I braced myself. I felt nauseous. I just knew the producers were going to show the "Christian Lady" yelling out an expletive. It would be the end of my ministry! It would make God look bad! He would be so disappointed in me!

And then...

Nothing.

They did not even show it on the air. They took it out completely. I was flabbergasted. In shock. All those hours and sleepless nights of worrying about how I was going to damage God's reputation and they didn't even show it. What was going on?

As I prayed about this with the Lord, I felt that what He was showing me is something He wants us all to know. We are human. We will mess up. We are not perfect (the very reason we need Jesus so much). And He showed me something that humbled me and will continue to humble me until the day I die: ***I am not powerful enough to ruin the God of the Universe's reputation.*** He's perfectly capable of protecting His honor. Even if they **had** shown me screaming out a word I would not normally use, God would have been just as holy. My actions proved I was human and I made a mistake, but they did nothing to discredit my God.

I do not know what you're struggling with today, my friend. But I know that if you are having a hard time letting go of the guilt, you need to remember that important truth. He loves you, He forgives you and He is not depending on you to be perfect in order to show others how amazing He is! Remember...*while we were yet sinners*, Christ died for us! He knows we are not perfect. As Jesus said to the woman who the judgmental Pharisees caught in adultery...*go and sin no more (John 8:1-11)*.

When you are exhausted, hungry for God's Word, thirsty for His Spirit and you're in a situation that is anything but what you are used to, you will be more vulnerable to do things you normally wouldn't do, too. It doesn't give us an excuse, but it certainly shows how much we depend on Him for our righteousness. And if you mess up, fess up. Learn, grow and move forward. Remember it, but don't dwell on it. As a Christian, we are a new creation, but sometimes our old self seeps out when we are in a vulnerable situation. Protect yourself from those situations whenever possible by staying in His Word, praying and allowing His Spirit to control you (Galatians 5:16).

When I told Courtney what I yelled out, her reaction wasn't one of, "Oh, I see. You say you're a Christian, but look at what you did!" It was more like this: "Oh, I see. You're human."

We are all human. You will make mistakes. Learn from them. Grow from them. Allow God to use the sins that you regret so much to teach you and form you into the person He wants you to be. But do not allow those sins to define you. Allow them to refine you. And move forward, in His grace. God's grace is always way bigger than the grace we show (or do not show) ourselves.

If you are a believer and you have sinned, you may feel like you have blown it and God is mad at you. Please know that there is forgiveness and restoration and even redemption for you! What I have learned from my experience is that when this happens (and believe me, it does), we have some steps we can take in order to restore our relationship with God and others:

- **Repent.** This means turn away from the sin and toward God, agree with God that it is sin and ask Him to forgive you. (Deal with it)
- **Receive.** Receive His forgiveness. Give yourself time to heal. Allow the sin to refine you, not define you. (Learn from it)
- **Revive.** Allow God to revive, or resurrect, your story and give a new life. What the enemy meant for harm, God can now use it for good. (Minister from it)
- **Rejoice!** Praise God and thank Him for this amazing gift of grace, forgiveness and restoration. (Find joy in spite of it)

Once I repented and received His forgiveness, I took time to heal and deal with my sin. God taught me so much through it. Eventually, He can use what I went through to minister to others as I am honest and open about my imperfectness. Sometimes that is not the case – sometimes it is a personal thing that God is just teaching me and He does not have me share it. He is very clear with me, what I must do. But I must be willing to allow Him to do whatever He needs to do through me. He is God and He knows best.

"Heart attacks" happen when you have your new heart. I have heard some preachers say that salvation makes your life so much better and that you'll be healthy, wealthy and better off once you get saved. I'm here to tell you that is not Biblical. Jesus tells us Himself that in this world, we will have trouble (not we *might*, but we *will*), but take heart; He has over come the world (John 16:33). It is not that our lives will be perfect with rainbows and butterflies, but we can always have peace that passes understanding in our times of trouble because He is always with us. We got through tough times, but we never go through them alone and there is always a greater purpose in our pain.

It's called *redemption*.

Chapter Fourteen

A Rejected Heart

He was despised and rejected— a man of
sorrows, acquainted with deepest grief.
We turned our backs on him and looked the other way.
He was despised, and we did not care. – Isaiah 53:3

How had I allowed it to come to this? I found myself ducking in the bushes outside of Bobby's dorm room, spying on him and his new girlfriend like some lovesick middle school girl. It was my second year of college and he and I had been dating for a while. He actually pursued me for weeks until I finally broke down and began to date him. He was a basketball player and I was a cheerleader. It was so perfect. We were "the" couple on campus and went everywhere together. I was so into him that when we broke up, not only did I lose a boyfriend, I also lost my dignity and any sense of pride that I ever had. I guess you could say I lost my mind.

I cried myself to sleep for months. I was obsessed with him and even though I thought I loved him, I began to hate him. I have actually heard that when you elevate a person in your life and put so much of your faith in them and then they (inevitably) let you down, that obsession turns to hate. I hated him, but only because he did not love me back. It was awful. Probably one of the worst feelings in all of my life. I never want to feel that way again.

In retrospect, I can honestly say that Bobby breaking up with me was the greatest thing that could have happened. Just a few short months later I met a guy named Rod Nease. We hit it off almost immediately and a year later we were married. If I had not been through that rejection, I never would have met my husband. Oh, thank God for that rejection! Remember how we talked about brokenness preceding usefulness with God? Well, I also believe that a broken heart is always followed up by a beautiful healing. God is so faithful.

Jeannie's new heart is something her body is not used to, so she has to monitor it constantly and take medication to keep her body from rejecting her new heart.. Recently, she was in the hospital for a couple of days because her heart was showing signs of rejection. During that time, she was ill, but in spite of that, she was also able to share her story and God's faithfulness with many people. She can now see that even during her heart's "rejection", God was faithful and He used her to show His grace and kindness to others through the experience.

Maybe there is someone in your life you recall rejecting you or breaking your heart. In retrospect, can you see yet how God had a better plan? I have come to realize in my life that man's rejection is always God's protection for me. God has a way of working things out for His glory and our good. It just does not always look like how we initially hope or think it should.

When you become a believer in Christ, you will find yourself in situations where you will be rejected for your faith in Him. Actually, He was rejected, too. The Jewish Pharisees rejected Him so much that they wanted Him crucified. If Jesus, Himself, was rejected, what makes us think we will never face it? He takes our rejection very personal, though. In the book of Acts, when Jesus revealed Himself to a Pharisee named Saul (who later became the Apostle Paul) who was persecuting Christians, He said, "Saul! Why are you persecuting me?" Notice, He said *me*. That is how personally He takes the persecution and insults hurled at believers for His sake. The insults that are thrown at us are also thrown at Him. We are now His – we have His heart.

Jesus also stated, in John 15:18-21, *"If the world hates you, remember that it hated me first. The world would love you as one of its own if you belonged to it, but you are no longer part of the world. I chose you to come out of the world, so it hates you. Do you remember what I told you? 'A slave is not greater than the master.' Since they persecuted me, naturally they will persecute you. And if they had listened to me, they would listen to you. They will do all this to you because of me, for they have rejected the one who sent me."*

If you are a people-pleaser and rejection bothers you, it is probably a good idea to give you a heads up that being a believer does not mean that you will be loved and accepted by everyone. Quite the contrary. Mark Burnett, the producer of *Survivor*, once said that when people who have achieved "life's ideal state" (in other words, believers) walk into a room full of unbelievers, the unbelievers feel quietly scorned for their imperfections; they feel judged, even if the believer doesn't say a word. It is, as he puts it, because so many people do not want to take the bold and difficult steps to make a change in their life, so they scorn those who do take those steps. That is why he likes to cast Christians on the show, *Survivor*. He likes to see the conflict that arises from internal struggles. There is a morality that is not easily tolerated by the majority of people because it brings on conviction and an uncomfortable feeling of being judged.

Maybe it is a person who does not agree with your beliefs rejecting you, but it could also be a job you keep applying for or a dream you keep chasing but never seem to be able to live out. Or perhaps it is another believer who is rejecting you. That is very difficult because we tend to put higher expectations on people who share our faith. But no matter what it looks like, rejection is a painful reality of life but God can use it for our good.

When I was voted off the reality show I was on in 2007, I remember feeling absolutely devastated. After my name was read and I was announced as the "third person to be voted out," I hugged all of my tribe mates, waved goodbye and walked off into the darkness with tears streaming down my face. What had I done wrong? Why me? How could I face my family after failing to make it very far in the game?

My thoughts were heavy and overwhelming as I rounded a corner and found one of the producers standing there waiting for me with a Coke and a Snickers bar! After nine days on the show and hardly anything to eat or drink, it was such a sight for sore eyes. I immediately grabbed it and chugged the Coke and downed the Snickers (we will not mention the belch that followed…). All of a sudden I realized I was not so upset anymore. Later, I was able to eat a full meal and take a shower for the first time in nine days. It was heavenly!

The next day I realized I had lost seventeen pounds during the time I was on the show and I was very sick. Physically, I doubt I could have lasted much longer out there, and God knew that. He protected me and when I realized that, I was not so upset anymore. God was in control and I put my faith in that fact. It eased my hurting heart and gave me strength to pull myself together. Instead of focusing on why I was rejected, I began to focus on living for the moment and asked God to give me opportunities to share my faith and His love with others. It was truly an amazing transition from feeling hopeless and rejected to feeling loved and protected.

When I first surrendered my life to Christ, I also faced some rejection from some of my former friends. I used to drink and party a lot and had quite a few friends whom I would party with. Once I became a Christian, my passions changed and as a result I did not have as much in common with them anymore. I began to realize I was not being invited to as many parties and found out that some of them were talking about me, calling me a "Jesus Freak" and commenting on how I had gone off the deep end. Most of them were supportive, but there were some that I still could not find common interests with, no matter how hard I tried.

It was not long after that, I read what Peter wrote in 1 Peter

4:2-5, *"You won't spend the rest of your lives chasing your own desires, but you will be anxious to do the will of God. You have had enough in the past of the evil things that godless people enjoy—their immorality and lust, their feasting and drunkenness and wild parties, and their terrible worship of idols.*

Of course, your former friends are surprised when you no longer plunge into the flood of wild and destructive things they do. So they slander you. But remember that they will have to face God, who will judge everyone, both the living and the dead."

What an incredible reminder this was that the most important thing for me to do was to stand firm in my faith because eternity is at stake. We will all have to face God one day, and I do not take that lightly. The witness my life gave off may not have been what some wanted to hear or see, but God may use it to change someone's heart. The rejection was a weapon the enemy would use to try to get me to compromise, but God used it for my good and taught me so much through it.

In 2 Corinthians 2:15-16, Paul reminds us that, *"Our lives are a Christ-like fragrance rising up to God. But this fragrance is perceived differently by those who are being saved and by those who are perishing. To those who are perishing, we are a dreadful smell of death and doom. But to those who are being saved, we are a life-giving perfume."*

Though to some, my life was now a "dreadful smell of death and doom," I had to remind myself that to others, including God Himself, my life was a pleasing perfume. It is like a "spiritual body odor" I suppose you could say. Now, over ten years later, some of those friends have a relationship with Christ. I am sad the rejection had to happen, but I am thankful God gave me the strength to remain steadfast in my faith in spite of the hurt and pain in my heart. Eventually, He brought new friends into my life and I was still able to love my old friends, it just looked different now that I was not the same person.

Rejection is not the end of the world, though it might feel like it at the moment of being rejected. God can use it to steer our lives in the direction He wants us to go. It is painful, but doesn't the thought of being in a destructive or toxic relationship or situation sound so much more excruciating?

Chapter Fifteen

Heart Overflow

A good person produces good things from the treasury of a good heart, and an evil person produces evil things from the treasury of an evil heart. What you say flows from what is in your heart. Luke 6:45

My sister and I were playing hopscotch on the driveway one sunny, hot day when we were very young. I said a word that I should not have said and she immediately ran into the house yelling, "Mom! Leslie said a bad word!" I knew I was in big trouble. We did *not* say that word in our family.

A few moments later, my sister comes outside, dragging my mother by the hand. I looked at my mom's face of disappointment and hung my head low. She seemed horrified. "Leslie, your sister tells me you said the F word. Is this true?" I did not even look up. I sheepishly replied, "Yes, ma'am. It's true." She looked even more disappointed and asked a follow up question, "Where on earth did you learn that word?" I shrugged my shoulders and told her I did not know where I had heard it. I just did. And I was sorry. She then said, "Leslie, I want you to spell the word for me so I know for sure it is the word I think it is." At first I said no, out of fear that she would be even more disappointed. But after her insisting, I finally caved in and began my dreadful spelling of the word we never, ever were allowed to say in our house. "Ok, mommy. F...A...R...T."

A look of complete and utter thrill washed over my mom's face and she almost seemed relieved. How could this be? She smiled very big and even giggled and then walked out of the garage saying, "Ok, sweetie, don't ever say it again!" That was it. No soap washing in my mouth. No spanking or restriction. Nothing!

It was not until I was much older that I realized why she let me off easy that day. I can honestly say now that I'm a mom that I would be relieved, too! It's a funny story to recall, but it reminds me of something not so funny.

When our children say bad words, we tend to want to wash their mouths out with soap so they will never say it again. Is this the right thing to do, though? Isn't it really their *heart* that needs a good washing? According to Jesus, what is in the heart overflows out of the mouth (Luke 6:45). We can tell a lot about what is going on in our hearts by the words that we speak.

I once heard an interesting Indian tale about a grandfather and grandson who were out hunting early one morning. They came upon a ridge on the mountain and as they were looking over the ridge, they could see two wolves - a black one, and a white one - fighting furiously.

The grandfather looked his grandson in the eyes with a very serious look, and said slowly, "Ah, yes, this is the way with all of us human beings within our hearts, each and every day." The grandson asked, "What do you mean, grandfather?" The old man replied, "Always in our hearts, every day, a fierce battle takes place just like those two wolves down there. One is the wolf in us who wishes to do bad things, and the other is the wolf who wishes to do good and honorable things." The grandson listened more intently now.

The grandfather continued, "Sometimes, the bad wolf seems to win, and other times, the good wolf seems to take a stronger lead. Each good and honorable deed he does gives his goodness more power within him. This in turn, empowers the human being to be more honorable." The boy smiled, as the grandfather continued to speak, "But when we see those people who turn to badness, and hatred, doing terrible and dishonorable things, we can know that the bad wolf within him is strong – and each bad and wrongful deed he does, gives the bad wolf more power over him, until it has won, and has utterly consumed him."

The young boy's face fell with a look of slight, shuddering inner fear. The boy thought long and hard on these things, as he continued to watch the wolves battling below. They both battled fiercely, neither one backing down. "But grandfather," said the boy, "How will I know which wolf will win within me? "The grandfather smiled, looked at him with an understanding eye, and after a moment, told him, "The one you *feed*."

What a great story. Of course, we know as believers that our "good wolf" is the power of Christ in us – the Holy Spirit – sent to lead us into the truth. He produces good things in us.

Our "bad wolf" is our flesh – our own desires that entice us and try to drag us away from what God wants for us. If we feed Christ in us by spending time in His word, acting in obedience, spending time with godly people and praying daily, we will find that our new heart will get stronger and stronger. If we feed our "bad wolf", or our flesh, by watching filthy movies, reading ungodly things or only spending time with people who do not love God and have no moral compass, we are going to be consumed by the evil. Again, as mentioned so many times, we have a choice. Our words and actions will eventually reveal what choice we have made.

Ask yourself some serious questions for a moment: What is coming out of my mouth these days? Where is it coming from? For instance...

- If it's gossip – could I have issues with pride or confidence?
- If it's angry words – could I have issues with bitterness in my heart?
- If it is dirty jokes – what could I be exposing myself to that is bringing this out of my heart?
- If it is resentful or hurtful words – could I be harboring a grudge or unforgiveness?
- If it is slander – could I have issues with jealousy or discontentment?

The root of what comes out of your mouth can always be traced back to something deeper in your heart. You have probably heard the saying, "Hurt people hurt people." It can be very true. If we have been hurt or offended, sometimes we can end up being hurtful and offensive. It is as if we try to protect our hearts from being hurt again by keeping people at a distance. The underlying issue can be so much deeper than we could ever imagine.

Maybe none of these describe you but you can think of someone in your life that displays these "symptoms" of a diseased spiritual heart. If so, does this help you understand them a little bit better? I sure hope so. When we begin to understand that what flows out of a mouth comes from the heart, it can be convicting for us but it can also be very insightful as we deal with others. We should not take things so personal when people are not always pleasant with us. It may have nothing to do with us at all.

There are going to be days when you feel like you are doing "pretty well" spiritually and then, "Wham!" you will realize you are in a not-so-well day all of a sudden. I know this because I experience it frequently. I'll give you a little insight into one of those moments that some overflow came out of my heart that I was not very proud of...

It was one of those mornings. I was doing just fine initially. I had a great quiet time, began my day by waking my daughters with sweet butterfly kisses, began to pick up little things here and there...and then it happened.

My youngest daughter yells out,"You never do laundry! I don't have a clean undershirt!" Just then, the dog barked. Nobody had let him out yet and his water and food were completely empty. I had to let him out. I promise you, if not for me, that poor dog would die of neglect. Then my other daughter started complaining about not having clean and matching socks, I realized I had three loads of laundry that were clean but sitting in various corners of my home waiting to be folded, I had to step over my son who fell asleep in the living room the night before, if I didn't clean my bathroom soon, I was sure social services would be here to give me a citation, I had a sink full of dishes and I promise you I think it had to be my worse hair day ever.

I couldn't resist it one more minute. I completely snapped. I let 'em have a piece of my very irritated mind: "I'm the only one who does anything around here! I didn't realize I was your personal slave! Maybe if you would gather up your dirty laundry and bring it down - maybe then you'd have clean undershirts! I don't have any socks either because you take all of my clean socks out of my drawer when you can't find yours and they disappear into oblivion somewhere! Someone's gonna catch something in that bathroom! Can I get some help around here for crying out loud? Today after school, it's ON TIL THE BREAK OF DAWN! You kids are cleaning and organizing and helping me get this house in order! I'm over it! No playing today, no fun 'til the work is done!" (hmm...remember, my husband used to say that?)

As I stormed around the house, picking things up (I do this when I am upset – I cannnot control it – it is like I turn into a little cleaning tornado) I began to ask God to help me. I knew I had blown it. All the quiet time words of wisdom were gone. I think they went into the oblivion my socks go into. Then I heard a still voice in my heart say, "Resist the devil and he will flee from you."

I can honestly tell you that there was a very big part of me that thought, "You know, I don't feel like resisting right now!" But as I sat there, folding one of my loads of laundry,

I began to pray. "God, please help me right now. I am angry, I am bitter and I am in a funk. I cannnot do this." Just then, my husband who had been observing my not so pleasant morning, approached me and put a book in my lap that was opened to a page that said, "Never, never, never give up." And the Scripture that was with this quote was Galatians 6:9, *"And let us not grow weary while doing good, for in due season we shall reap if we do not lose heart."*

My perspective began to change as the Lord brought to mind my friend, Julia. She had laundry, two boys, a husband, cleaning, cooking, a full time job and two dogs to care for and she did it all while going through chemotherapy – for years and years. And she did it praying all the while that the Lord would give her time to continue to serve her family in this way. Oh, wow, I was feeling conviction now.

It was not that my kids did not deserve to be disciplined, because they certainly did. However, my tone with them was a true indication that my heart was not healthy at that moment. I was allowing the built up resentment and bitterness to overflow onto my family and it was wrong. Later that day, I apologized and we had a very civil talk about how things needed to change.

I would venture to say we have all had moments like that; when we mess up and say things we really wish we had not said in a tone we wish we had not used. It usually happens when we have not dealt with things in our hearts the way God would have had us to deal with them. It is a symptom of "heart disease" I suppose you could say.

A great way to try to overcome this is to frequently ask God to reveal those things that are storing up in your heart that are not healthy. Things you need to confess. Things you need to deal with. People you need to forgive. Words you need to say. Confrontation that you must face (if you're like me this is tough – I hate confrontation). No matter what it is, God will be faithful to reveal it to you. Your job is to be faithful in dealing with it.

King David prayed a powerful prayer about his "heart sins" when, in Psalm 19:12-14, he wrote, *"How can I know all the sins lurking in my heart? Cleanse me from these hidden faults. Keep your servant from deliberate sins! Don't let them control me. Then I will be free of guilt and innocent of great sin. May the words of my mouth and the meditation of my heart be pleasing to you, O Lord, my rock and my redeemer."* Now that prayer is a great place to start. This is something we can all pray each day and know beyond a shadow of a doubt that God will answer. It is in His Word and His Word is trustworthy and true.

I want to encourage you to give yourself time with your new spiritual heart. Just like in Jeannie's heart transplant, it takes awhile for your new heart to become fully functioning. Celebrate the small victories, and try not to be so hard on yourself when you do mess up from time to time. God does not expect you to be perfect. He already knows you aren't – that's why He sent Jesus! He just wants you to be more like Christ, and your sin now refines you, remember? It no longer has the power to define you.

Jeannie Fuller knew that when she received her new heart, life would never again be the same. She had no idea the incredible lessons God would show her as a result of this gift of life He provided through her precious donor. She learned to appreciate each day more, she learned to be faithful in the small things she had to do to keep her heart healthy, she learned to be patient and to allow time for her heart to get stronger and more steady. Jeannie learned so much and I have learned so much from watching her that I can apply to my life as a spiritual heart recipient.

If you have read this entire book and still have not had your own spiritual heart transplant, I want to encourage you to spend some time, one on one, with God. Read through the book of Luke in the New Testament and ask God to reveal Himself to you. He says over and over again, "If you seek me with all of your heart, you will find me." I pray that you will find Him as you seek Him with all of your heart! You are in my prayers and I am so honored you would spend some time with me in the pages of this book.

I cannot believe our time together is drawing to an end! What an incredible journey this has been for me, and I pray it has been for you, as well. Before I close, I want to leave you with some encouragement from Romans 15:13. Paul wrote this to the Romans, and I could not have said it better myself:

I pray that God, the source of hope, will fill you completely with joy and peace because you trust in Him. Then you will overflow with confident hope through the power of the Holy Spirit.